D0908803

Positive Shooting

Positive Shooting

MICHAEL YARDLEY

The Crowood Press

First published in 1993 by
The Crowood Press Ltd
Ramsbury, Marlborough
Wiltshire SN8 2HR

British Library Cataloguing-in-Publication Data
A catalogue record for this book is available from the British Library.

ISBN   1 85223 749 X

Dedication
For my children

Photographs and line-drawings by the author except where indicated
otherwise.

Throughout this book, 'he', 'him' and 'his' have been used as neutral
pronouns and refer to both sexes.

Typeset by Inforum, Rowlands Castle, Hants
Printed and bound in Great Britain by
BPCC Hazell Books Ltd
Member of BPCC Ltd

Contents

Acknowledgements

Anyone who has set out to write a book will know that it usually takes longer than expected and requires forbearance from friends and family. I take this opportunity to thank all those who have sustained, encouraged or advised me during the last three years. I could not have finished this project without their help and am especially grateful to: Elizabeth Mallard-Shaw, John and Vivien Yardley, Richard and Alastair Ford, Andrew Perkins, Morlin Ellis, Trevor Scott, Bob Clarke, John Rosenberg, Tony Morris, Fiona Yardley, Alan Rhone, Richard Law, Dick Ward, Jan Stevenson, Ian Cawthorne, Ray Hulston, Alex Foley, Emilio Orduna, Carl Bloxham, Steve and Mark Senn, Alan and Michael Rose, John Bidwell, Judith White, Trevor Booker, Nigel Teague, Paul Roberts, Piers Crump, Paul Bentley, Andrew Young, David Peel, Gordon Swatton, Brian Hebditch, Bob Frampton, Malcolm Grendon and Mark Course, Garry Coward-Williams, R.J. Pitcher, Bernard Cole, Robin Scott, Mike George, Professor Ariel Lant, and Kevin Gill.

There are many others too, not least all those people I have shot with over the years and from whom I have learnt so much. I also owe a debt to the great shots whose work has much influenced my own, most notably Percy Stanbury, H.A. Thorne (Charles Lancaster), and Robert Churchill. There are others whose expertise is well recognized and whose work has affected my own: Major Sir Gerald Burrard, Gough Thomas, Bob Brister, W.W. Greener, Elmer Keith and Chris Craddock immediately come to mind. I have also enjoyed and learnt from the books of Paul Bentley, A.J. Smith, Art Blatt, J.E.M. Ruffer, Kay Ohye, G.T. Teasdale Buckell, T.D.S. and J.A. Purdey, Barney Hartman, Ed Sherer, Don Zutz, John Linn and Stephen Blumenthal, Geoffrey Boothroyd, Ken Davies, Richard Akehurst, John Brindle, Richard Arnold, Bruce Bowlen, Arthur Hearn, Mike Reynolds, and Wayne Martin.

Finally, I would thank all my students. Ultimately this is their book; it is a product of what they have taught me.

Introduction

The primary aim of *Positive Shooting* is to improve your shotgun marksmanship. The text is orientated towards the discipline of Sporting Clays, but the principles set out might usefully be applied to most sorts of shotgunning.

Why yet another book on shooting? A great deal has been written over the years about shotgun technique: some of it is very good but, sadly, much is not. There is far too much opinion and prejudice dressed up as fact. Everyone seems to say, 'My way is best'. I hope that I have not fallen into that trap here. I do present my own method of shooting, but a number of other methods are also discussed, because to shoot really well at Sporting targets requires mastery of more than one technique. What the shooter needs – and what he is given in this book – is a sound and simple core technique, awareness of other techniques which may be considered once the basic technique (applicable to 90 per cent of targets) is learnt well and, most importantly, a positive approach to shooting which will improve performance whatever the specific technique or style being used.

Essentially, Positive Shooting is a distillation of those things which have improved my own shooting over the past twenty years, and which I have also found useful in improving the shooting of others. There may not be many revelations here (although I hope there is one or two) but there are a number of tried and tested ideas which, when applied to your shooting, can help you perform more effectively. If I were pressed to identify a single special feature of the Positive Shooting approach, it would be its focus on mental discipline: the integration of mental and physical skills into a complete technique.

Positive Shooting lays great emphasis on structured practice; it also recognizes the importance of the individual's understanding as precisely as possible what he ought to be doing, physically and mentally. The goal here is increased self-awareness. Self-knowledge precedes improvement. As far as the actual process of shooting is concerned (as opposed to all the training and preparation which must precede it) the Positive Shooting technique might be summed up thus:

Every time you shoot at a clay target, make a special effort to study its line and speed. Establish: (a) where you first see the target as a blur or streak; (b) where you first see it clearly as a solid object; and (c) that place along the line of flight where it may most easily be shot – the 'killing point'. Set up your stance according to the chosen killing point. Mount the gun (rules permitting) on that killing point and visualize the target breaking; wind back along the line of flight. Stop at the point of first clear visual contact. Lower the butt out of the shoulder, but keeping the muzzles just under the line of flight. Direct the eyes by turning the head slightly to the area where the target is first seen as a blur or streak. Call for the target. Lock your eyes onto its leading edge.

If you do these things habitually, react well to the target and maintain visual contact, I guarantee your scores will improve. I do not advocate a conscious system of forward allowance for *most* targets because it makes shooting more complicated than it needs to be and can fail dismally on deceptive angles. However, experiment has taught me that the unconscious approach to lead will work reliably only if you prepare yourself properly (with the aid of a simple but specific and consciously applied pre-shooting routine) and maintain visual contact. All this said, I accept that there are some people who need to apply lead deliberately, and some targets which favour a more deliberate approach. Nothing in shooting is written in stone; ultimately, what is right is what works for you.

In this book, safety is the subject of the first chapter because my own experience is that most of us are not as safe as we should like to think. I then look at the various Sporting disciplines and gun selection before going on to technique. I have also included a catalogue of specific tips for specific birds, and chapters on the psychology of shooting and physical fitness, and gunfit. The essence of Positive Shooting is found in Chapters 4 and 5; less experienced shooters would be well advised to concentrate on them and on the safety section of Chapter 1.

Because there is so much information presented here, there may also be the potential to confuse or distract. To help you find your way through the book I shall list the priorities of the aspiring Sporting shot thus:

1. Safe gun handling.
2. Good basic technique (and especially a good gun mount).
3. A well-fitted gun (which becomes even more important as ability grows).
4. Experience of different targets.

Once the shooter has learnt to respect the potential danger of firearms, by far the most important skill to develop is a good gun mount. This is the foundation upon which all consistent shooting is based. When I hold Positive Shooting courses, much time is spent on this aspect of basic technique.

Moreover, it would be a great mistake to think that attention to gun mount or to other aspects of basic technique is something to be restricted to those in the early stages of learning. Far from it. One former World Sporting Champion told me recently that he practised his mount every day and had done so for the last twenty years. You may not have that dedication, but the importance of a good mount cannot be overstressed; it might be compared to the swing in golf or the seat in riding. Attention to the basics pays great dividends in all sports; it is vitally important to the shooter who wants to discover his true potential.

In conclusion, perhaps the main reason I was motivated to write *Positive Shooting* was the observation that many shooters have never really learnt the basics of their sport adequately. They have a sloppy approach. In many cases it is not their own fault, but a result of the rather unstructured way we set about shooting instruction in the UK. This lack of clear method concerns me, and has coaxed me into putting pen to paper. Whether you aspire to break a few more birds at your club or to win major competitions, I hope *Positive Shooting* will help you to improve your performance by giving you a clearer understanding of what it is you ought to be doing *and* thinking when you shoot.

Michael Yardley, Essex, 1993

1 Safety

I have seen someone shot; I hope you never do. People get killed every year with Sporting shotguns. This is not to say that clay, and, indeed, game shooting are not safe sports. They are, statistically, very safe: safer than football or fishing. But they are also potentially lethal, which is why all shooters must take the special responsibility of their sport very seriously. You cannot say sorry to a corpse. If you want to shoot well, you must first acquire the discipline to shoot safely.

Never point a gun at something you are not willing to destroy.

THE ABC OF SAFETY

A A closed shotgun is always treated as if it were loaded. Why? People get killed by 'empty' guns every year. Whenever you close the action of a gun, think about controlling where you point the muzzles. You must develop 'muzzle awareness', the mind-set that makes sure the muzzles are *always* pointing in a safe direction. Muzzle awareness is the first and last line of defence against shooting accidents.

B When you are not shooting, or about to shoot, your gun's action should be open, and when you carry your gun at a clay-pigeon shoot, you should do so with the action 'broken' or locked back. Break-action guns should be carried barrels forward, resting on the forearm (the best choice), or barrels forward, resting on your shoulder and secured with one hand. Semi-automatics and pump-

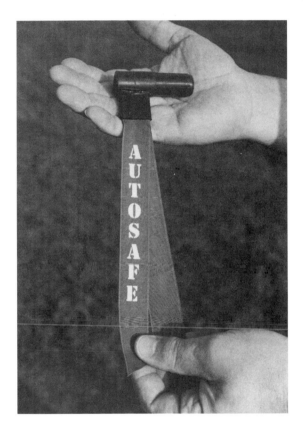

A safety plug and streamer for a semi-automatic or pump-action gun.

action guns should be carried either under the arm with the muzzles pointing at about 45 degrees towards the ground or, better, with the muzzles (the end of the barrels) pointing straight up, as a soldier marches with a rifle. It is also a courtesy to other shooters to place a handkerchief or specially made safety plug with streamer in the open ejection port of repeaters.

Safe ways of carrying guns while clay shooting. The preferred way of carrying break-action guns is resting on the forearm.

C Always check or 'prove' a gun empty, and check that the barrels are unobstructed (break-action guns) when it is passed to you, when you pick it up, or when you pass it to someone else. With semi-automatics, always check that the magazine tube as well as the chamber is unloaded.

LOADING

The gun should be loaded only when one is in the designated firing position or cage (the barrels should always be over the front bar of the cage – if it has one – when loading).

Before loading, always look down the barrels of a break-action gun to check for obstructions, such as mud in the muzzles or a smaller-bore cartridge which might have fallen down the barrels. One classic accident involves confusing 12- and 20-bore cartridges, inserting a 20-bore

When you pick up a gun, ALWAYS check that it is unloaded and unobstructed.

The dramatic result of confusing 12- and 20-bore cartridges.

Another spectacular barrel burst caused by an obstruction halfway down the barrels of a side-by-side. Note how thin the barrel walls are.

Always be aware of the danger of confusing 12- and 20-bore cartridges. If you have both types of gun, the best thing to do is keep separate cartridge bags. When you have finished shooting, always check your pockets too.

cartridge in a 12-bore chamber, and then loading a 12-bore cartridge on top. This effectively turns the breech of the gun into a hand-grenade next to the shooter's face and hands. If you shoot a 20-bore, but normally use a 12, always double check your pockets after shooting. If you routinely use both types of gun, keep separate cartridge bags for each bore size. Similar precautions must be taken when using a 28 with a 20.

When taking guns out of slips, make sure they are 'broken' before being fully removed, and get in the habit of extending the trigger finger along the trigger guard at all times when handling a gun. Think about this; watch others. You will be surprised at how bad most people's gun-handling is.

Do not be afraid to tell others if they are handling guns dangerously, but always be polite. If they do not respond, get away from them as fast as possible. If someone mentions a point of safety to you, do not take it as an insult, thank them for the observation. We are all capable of making mistakes. I admit that I

When you take a gun out of the slip, keep your finger on the trigger guard and break the gun before withdrawing it.

have made them. When you realize that an accident *can* happen to you, you are the sort of person with whom others will want to shoot.

HOW TO CLOSE A GUN

When closing a break-action gun, or bringing the action forward on semi-automatic or pump-action types, always make sure that your finger is off the trigger and the muzzles are pointing in a safe direction (ideally, at 45 degrees to the ground in front of you). Then if it does accidentally go off, it will do no great damage.

Always close a gun with firm but gentle control. *Never* slam it shut: a protruding firing pin

can cause an accidental discharge. This is my normal procedure for closing a break-action gun:

1.   Make sure the gun is pointing in a safe direction and that the barrels are not obstructed.
2.   Stand with the left foot at one o'clock and the right foot at approximately three o'clock, heels about six inches (15 cm) apart (mirror image for left-handers). Hold the butt of the open gun gently wedged between forearm and rib-cage and slightly canted clockwise (anti-clockwise for left-handers). Extend the trigger finger along the trigger guard.
3.   Grip the gun firmly with the right hand, and lean forward slightly.
4.   Bring the barrels up with the left hand, while at the same time pushing down on the top of the grip with the right hand. The action will close.

Throughout the process, the muzzles are carefully controlled so they continue to point in a safe direction. Pick up a gun, and try this procedure now. In the case of semi-automatics and pumps, a similar system may be adopted: with any gun, what counts is firm control and awareness that the muzzles are pointing in a safe direction as the action is closed. People will judge you on your gun-handling. Take a pride in it.

The traditional way to close a double gun is to 'bring the stock and action to the barrels', in other words to hold the fore-end with the front hand whilst pushing the stock up at wrist or heel. This method is fine in experienced hands (and the best way to close a gun when one is in a cage with a high front bar – *see* note below), but beginners tend to lose control of the muzzles as the stock is pushed up because the gun rotates about the axis of their weak hand. Nevertheless, get your gun and try to close it this way as well. Keep practising until you feel comfortable with the technique; you will need to use it sometimes.

My preferred method of closing a break-action gun, as described in the text. A faulty technique can leave the gun pointing at your feet.

Note: Never close a gun with the barrels pointing anywhere inside the cage. One sometimes sees people doing this, and then lifting the loaded gun so that the barrels are directed above the front bar. This is a very dangerous habit because the movement is awkward and it is possible to lose one's grip on the gun. It does not take much imagination to appreciate the possible consequences if a loaded gun should be dropped with its barrels pointing upwards.

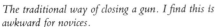

The traditional way of closing a gun. I find this is awkward for novices.

SAFETY CATCHES

I have made no mention so far of the safety catch. The reason for this is simple enough: the safety catch has no place in clay shooting. Safety in clay shooting relies on two things essentially: a system of checks, which makes sure the gun is unloaded at all times — except when it is actually being used on the firing point — and an unbreakable rule that guns are always pointed in a safe direction. Safety catches (and the phrase is misleading because many safety catches are no more than trigger blocks — the gun can go off even with the safety catch applied) have a place in game shooting, but serve no useful purpose on a competition gun. Some shooters choose to have them locked into firing position by a gunsmith. This is not my own

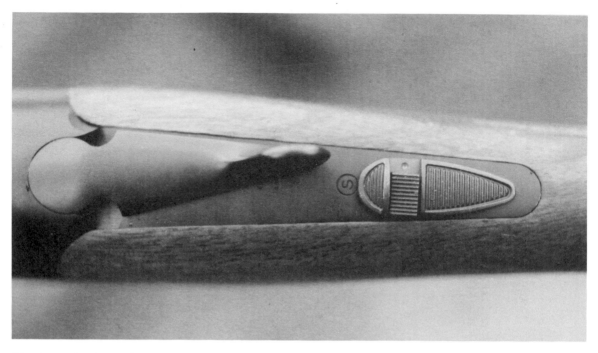

The safety catch. This one, like many on over-and-unders, incorporates a barrel-selector.

preference, but there is no reason why it should not be done. Automatic safety catches (the type that is automatically applied when the gun is opened) are definitely a nuisance in competitive shooting and may usually be converted to manual operation by a competent gunsmith.

CONDUCT ON THE FIRING POINT

Load the gun only after you are in the designated firing position and with the muzzles pointed in a safe direction. When you have finished shooting, check that the gun is unloaded and unobstructed. Never turn to leave the firing point before doing these things.

You will observe many shooters (who, no doubt, would swear that they are safe), loading their guns just a litle earlier than they should and failing to prove their gun empty before leaving the firing position.

MISFIRES

Occasionally you will come across a defective cartridge. Usually the only problem will be a failure to go off because of a faulty or incorrectly positioned primer. Misfires are usually no more than an inconvenience, and are easily remedied (unless caused by a fault in the gun's mechanism) by replacing the faulty cartridge with another one. However, you should always wait 30 seconds after a misfire before opening the gun. And when you do open the gun, the chamber mouths should be directed away from the face. Very occasionally, what appears to be a misfire may actually be a 'hangfire' – a delayed ignition of the propellant powders. To open the gun in these circumstances risks the cartridge going off without the restraint of the breech, a situation definitely to be avoided.

Another situation where a little common sense must be applied is when the cartridge fires as the trigger is pulled, but with a muffled

A young shooter being taught good habits. Notice that he holds the gun at approximately a 45-degree angle to the ground as his father watches carefully.

report instead of the normal loud bang. If, on pulling the trigger, the detonation sounds in any way odd, wait for a moment. When you do open the gun, check to see that the barrels are unobstructed by the wadding or anything else. If you do not check for obstructions after a muffled report (or indeed, routinely before loading as already suggested) you may well end up with a gun with bulged or burst barrels.

Another cartridge failure worth mentioning is case separation. In its most dangerous form, everything sounds normal after firing, but only the rim of the cartridge is ejected from the gun. The plastic (or paper) section of the case detaches itself from the rim, and lodges in the forcing cone (the funnel-like constriction immediately in front of the chambers) or in the bore. This is potentially hazardous because it creates an obstruction. The moral here, and indeed in all things concerned with safety, is: 'Expect the unexpected'.

The result of a case separation.

PROOF

Proof is another important aspect of gun safety. The origins of firearm proof testing are similar to the origins of the system for the hallmarking of gold and silver – it is a guarantee of quality, imposed on the gun trade by the master gunsmiths, and now enshrined in law in the UK by the Gun Barrel Proof Act of 1868 and the Rules of Proof, 1989 (which now supplant the rules of 1954). All guns sold in Britain must have been proof tested with an especially powerful proof charge. All new guns sold in Britain have either been proofed here by one of the two proof houses (one is in London, the other in Birmingham), or by a recognized proof house in another country which is a member of the International Proof Commission, such as those in Germany, Belgium, Italy, France and Spain. There is no equivalent of national proof in the United States or Japan for Sporting guns, where manufacturers test their own products. Thus guns coming into the UK from America or Japan must be proofed in London or Birmingham before retail sale.

Guns can also go 'out of proof' (and require reproofing which they may pass or fail) because of deliberate enlargement to the bore during a repair process, or because they have worn. Before the introduction of the current proof rules, which are oriented towards a metric system, British 12-bore guns were usually made with a

Proof marks on a Spanish gun. Most guns will include proof and makers' marks to tell you the chamber size, the level of pressure to which they have been proofed, the bore size (for example, a 12-bore gun might be marked 18.3, 18.4, 18.5 or 18.6mm), and the degree of choke constriction.

Various stages of the proof procedure being carried out at the London Proof House.

A gunsmith examines the bores of a gun by sight.

bore diameter of about .729in and went out of proof when they reached .740in. The new proof regulations have done more than merely change from imperial to a metric system; proof marks for pressure now show the Minimum Proof Loading, rather than the Highest Mean Service Pressure as was previously the case. There are other significant changes, but they go beyond the scope of this book. Readers who are interested should order a copy of *Notes on the Proof of Shotguns and other Small Arms* available from the London Proof House or the Birmingham Proof House (*see* Useful Addresses). A full account of the latest regulations is also available from either Proof House, or from Her Majesty's Stationary Office (*see* Further Reading).

From our point of view, a shooter has, primarily, two questions to consider regarding proof. Both are important for his own safety:

1. Is the gun in proof?
2. Have I selected the right cartridge? Many older English guns are proofed for a 2½in (65mm) cartridge and must never – if so marked – be used with the more modern 2¾in (70mm) loads *even though these may fit in the chamber*. Some old guns are proofed only for black powder; they should never be used with modern cartridges, without being subject to reproofing. If you have any doubts regarding proof or the suitability of a particular cartridge for your gun, go to an established gunsmith or firearms dealer and ask. Never take a risk.

Semi Automatics and Pump Guns

If you want to possess a semi-automatic or pump-action shotgun on a shotgun certificate in the UK, it must have been converted, or manufactured, to hold no more than two cartridges in the magazine tube. If the gun has been converted (usually by crimping the magazine tube), it must also be proof-stamped, and should, technically, have a proof certificate to this effect.

Sleeved Barrels

After the last war, a clever method of restoring side-by-side shotgun barrels was invented called sleeving. It involves cutting off the old barrels just ahead of the chambers, and, after counterboring, inserting new barrel tubes into the remaining breech assembly. It is similar, but not as strong as, the 'monobloc' process used to build most mass-produced over-and-unders today (in this process, two barrel tubes are inserted into a purpose-built breech block made from a single piece of steel). The great advantage of sleeving is that the original ejectors, rib and barrel lump may be reused. It is a much simpler, and cheaper, process than making completely new barrels. Consequently, many thousands of old English guns have been restored to shooting condition by this method.

A gun that has been sleeved must be reproofed, and stamped 'sleeved'. Because it affects originality and, insignificantly, the strength of the barrels, sleeving depresses the

Loading the semi-automatic. The action is locked back, one cartridge is dropped into the chamber, the working parts are allowed to come forward and the second cartridge is loaded into the magazine.

value of a gun. Moreover, there have been a few occasions when the unscrupulous have (illegally) effaced the special proof markings in order to pass the gun off as being in unusually good condition for its age. When buying any used gun, it is wise to check the external (and internal) finish of the barrels very carefully. Refinished barrels should always set the alarm bells ringing, as indeed should immaculate bores on an older gun. Are the barrels sleeved? Have they been lapped out (enlarged to remove imperfections)? Have they been otherwise repaired? On older game guns, barrels were sometimes re-blacked to disguise the fact that they were made originally with Damascus steel. This kind of camouflaging is less common now that collectors appreciate the beauty of twist steel barrels.

A SOUND GUN

If you have doubts about the serviceability of a gun, have it checked by a reputable dealer or gunsmith. It may, however, be useful to know some basic characteristics of a gun in sound condition.

Barrels

A serviceable gun should have well-polished bores without severe pitting and should show no signs of dents in the bore or bulges on the outside of the barrel. Using a gun that has been dented or bulged (even slightly) is potentially dangerous to both you and the gun. A dent will result in weak spots developing in the barrel as the metal is stressed by the passage of wad and shot. Dents are easily repaired, as long as they are fresh; a dent which has been left and from which a bulge has developed is a much more expensive problem. If a gun gets dented in the course of a day's shooting, put it away even if the damage appears very slight.

If the barrels are removed from a serviceable gun, and are then held by the lump and tapped

---

Inspecting Barrels

Procedure for looking for internal barrel imperfections (from *Amateur Gunsmithing*, Desmond Mills and Mike Barnes, Boydell Press, 1986.):

Hold the barrels up at eye level at about 45 degrees and point towards a constant, diffused light source . . . do not point into the sun or an electric light which will dazzle your eyes. Position the tubes a few inches from your eyes and keep both eyes open . . . look into the barrels rather than through them. Pivoting the barrels on your left hand, which should be half-way up the tube, describe a shallow circle with the barrels. This will throw a shadow down the inside walls and betray any dents or rivelling. If you spot any suspicious marks, turn the barrels to different angles and concentrate your attention to that spot. View from both ends of the barrel to confirm the mark as dent, bulge or whatever . . .

---

gently with a pen or pencil, they should ring; if there is a dull sound or a tinny rattle, it is an indication of problems (although it may be nothing more than a loose rib).

There should be no obvious movement between barrels and action in a gun in sound condition. (To test for it, remove the fore-end of a proven empty gun, hold the muzzles up with one hand, secure the butt by squeezing it between the thighs, and apply sideways presure at the barrel/action joint with the free hand. If there is movement, it indicates that the gun is 'off the face' and requires rejointing to bring it back into serviceable condition.) A gun that is loose will recoil much more than it should. As long as these problems are caught early, they are not that difficult or expensive to put right. Do not use a gun that is off the face. Apart from the discomfort, the problem will become more expensive to rectify the more you use the gun. One otherwise excellent gun that often seems to shoot loose is the Winchester 101 over-and-under (and other guns based on the 101's action).

Trigger and Safety Catch

A gun in serviceable condition will have trigger pulls that are firm and crisp. Trigger 'creep' is a sign of poor workmanship, but may often be rectified by a good gunsmith. A gun in good condition will also have a functioning safety catch (unless it has been deliberately immobilized) as described earlier.

Stock

A serviceable gun will have no cracks in the stock. Examine the stock very carefully, preferably removed from the action. The head of the stock (where it makes contact with the rear of the action) and the grip are the places where cracks commonly occur. Cracks in the fore-end are also common, particularly in the areas where inletting for metal parts has taken place. As well as being on the lookout for cracks, you should also make sure that there are no obvious gaps between the action and the stock; look especially at the area on either side of the top strap. Any signs of splaying may indicate that the stock bolt is a poor fit and/or over-tightened.

Abuse

A serviceable gun usually looks well cared for externally and internally. The lump of the barrels and the knuckle and hinge-pin of the action are unlikely to show signs of abuse from hurried take-down or reassembly. One problem that afflicts a few modern, mass-produced guns is that the knuckles become prematurely worn because of poor machining on the surfaces of the knuckle. I have seen this on several guns recently; it may also be that there is some metallurgical problem. The knuckles of all guns should be kept clean and well lubricated.

A serviceable gun will not have deep rust on barrel or action (any rust is a sign of poor care).

Strikers

The strikers (firing pins) should have tips that are rounded and neither chipped nor mushroomed. If the strikers are damaged or worn, misfires will result.

Ejectors

The ejectors (which can be checked with snap caps) should be positive in action and well timed: they should throw out both cartridges simultaneously when the gun is opened.

Top Lever

The top lever should have no play in it, and should be well sprung, returning easily to its closed position, with no sign either of looseness or of stickiness.

Refinishing

Evidence of refinishing, such as very worn engraving on the barrel or action, should make you cautious. At the least, it is likely that the gun has been used a lot.

Incompetent Repair

Avoid guns with signs of incompetent repair or servicing, such as damaged screw heads or poor wood-to-metal or metal-to-metal fit.

Multichokes

Check that the choke tubes are easily removable, and that their threads and those in the barrel are in good condition. If the gun has been multichoked after manufacture, check that the choke tubes have not been dented and that sufficient 'meat' has been left in the muzzles.

Semi-Automatics

Check the action body carefully. The Remington 1100, an otherwise magnificent gun, does very occasionally crack at the rear of the slot cut for the cocking lever; that is the slot in the side of the action, which is an extension of the ejection port opening.

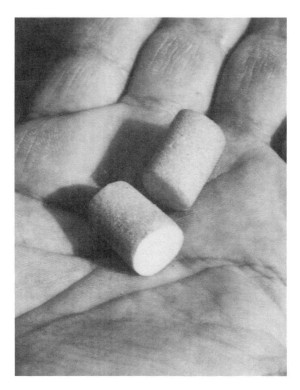

The commonly available, malleable, plastic plugs offer excellent protection at minimal cost.

Caveat Emptor

Finally, beware second-hand guns. Like second-hand cars, they can be made to look prettier and safer than they really are. To test definitively the condition of a gun requires great experience and specialist instruments to measure the size of the bore and the wall thickness of the barrels. Pitting or other damage may have been removed by 'lapping' inside the barrels. This is a normal repair procedure, but it can become a problem if carried to the point where barrel wall thickness is compromised. The golden rule is that if you are in any way unsure about a gun, take it to a reputable dealer for a check – if this is not acceptable to a private vendor, find another gun to buy.

PROTECT YOUR HEARING

Too many shooters still shoot without ear protection, even though it is proven that this will eventually cause deafness or tinnitus (constant ringing in the ears). Such shooters are foolish; there is nothing admirable about needlessly injuring yourself. To get technical for a moment, experts suggest that hearing protection must be worn whenever noise rises above 90 decibels. The impulse noise from shotguns can register anything up to 160 decibels. There is no question that hearing protection is required.

Any shooter can acquire good hearing protection, either muffs or plugs. I prefer the reasonably priced sponge or foam plugs. Surprisingly, they offer a high degree of protection and they cannot impede mounting. The type of ear-plugs moulded to fit the ear offer excellent protection, but they are expensive, and some people find them uncomfortable. A few shooters opt for muffs *and* plugs. In some shooting disciplines (trap shooting and pistol shooting, for example) a sense of isolation may improve performance. I prefer, in Sporting shooting, to keep hearing protection to the minimum *safe* level; I like to hear the traps being released.

Many shooting instructors now use the new electronic muffs, which are quite expensive but very effective in cutting out gun noise, and have the added advantage of allowing the wearer to hear normal speech and other background noise by means of a special amplifier. It is worth noting that the firer of a gun is actually exposed to less noise than someone standing

Effective hearing protection is essential. More and more shooters feel that eye protection is equally important. The muffs shown in this picture are the electronic type.

immediately to his or her side. Ultimately, your choice of hearing protection depends on what you feel comfortable with, as long as it exceeds the safety minimum. If you choose muffs, I suggest that before buying any, you try mounting a gun with them on – some types, on some shooters, hit the gun stock as it is brought to the face. If this happens, try another design. If you want to wear a hat or cap, you will need to take this into consideration when purchasing hearing protection.

PROTECT YOUR EYES

Few shooters in Britain who do not otherwise wear glasses bother with eye protection. Ear

protection is essential; eye protection may be as well – it is certainly prudent. Anyone learning to shoot should get into the habit of protecting his eyes from the start. Many shooting instructors now wear protective glasses all the time because they are dependent on their eyes for a living and know that eye injuries are relatively common in shooting. The right pair of glasses will offer protection against blowback from propellant gases (quite common in semi-automatic guns), stray pellets (Heaven forbid), and, the greatest hazard, bits of broken clay.

Additionally, glasses with special tints may also offer advantages on sunny or dull days. Yellow lenses are popular, and are meant to improve visibility and contrast on overcast days or towards dusk. Every serious Sporting shooter should also have a couple of pairs of sunglasses, a normal pair for bright conditions and an even darker pair for those occasions when he is forced to shoot directly into the sun (something to avoid whenever possible).

Protect Your Eyes

When shopping for glasses, make sure they are guaranteed impact-resistant, and keep them in a protective case to avoid the lenses getting scratched. If you can, get the hard type of case from an optician rather than a soft plastic slip, and keep a cloth with them so you can wipe any grease or finger prints off the lenses before shooting. Get in the habit of storing your glasses in your shooting bag or box.

GUN CLEANING

You might be surprised to find gun cleaning mentioned in a section on safety, but regular cleaning is an important safety consideration. It helps maintain guns in serviceable condition as long as possible and allows for a regular inspection of the gun. I can think of many occasions

Conventional cleaning equipment. Many shooters keep a cleaning rod in the back of the car.

when I have picked up problems like loose ribs or cracked stocks while cleaning, which I did not notice while shooting: it gets you in the habit of treating your gun with respect.

When you return from shooting you should take the barrels off the action and, using a cleaning rod or piece of dowelling, push some newspaper or kitchen towelling through the bores from the chamber end. Then scrub the barrels with a bronze brush, being particularly careful to remove the fouling in front of the chamber and at the chokes. Push through more paper until the bores are bright, and finish with a lightly oiled wool mop or patch. If the gun has a ventilated rib, a feather is invaluable for cleaning around the bridges; the feather will also be useful for cleaning around the extractors or ejectors of break-action guns.

The action of the gun should be wiped clean, paying special attention to the area around the striker holes, the bolting mechanism and the knuckle and hinge-pin. An old toothbrush may be used to clean out any debris in awkward places. The action may be lightly oiled after cleaning: many shooters use an aerosol spray. The gun should be wiped off after any oil has been sprayed on it, and it is sensible occasionally to put a little grease on the knuckle and hinge-pin. If a gun has multichokes fitted, it goes without saying that these should be removed and cleaned after each shooting session, paying particular attention to the threads on the chokes and inside the barrels.

Do not get into the habit of dismantling guns out of simple curiosity. But if a gun gets really wet and you are able to take the stock off and remove the locks without specialist skills, go ahead. Gun stocks should never be put away damp. If they do become wet, wipe them as dry as possible and let them dry out naturally for a few hours, then rub a little linseed oil thinned with turpentine into the wood. Be careful not to overdo the linseed oil: over-oiling a stock can clog the checkering and weaken the wood. Never heat guns to dry them.

Safety at Home

A large proportion of shooting accidents occur while cleaning guns, notably while cleaning supposedly unloaded guns at home. Do not forget the basic principles of safety just because you are relaxing at home. Before you start to clean a gun, make sure it is unloaded. If you put snap caps in a gun to ease the springs, make sure the muzzles are pointing at a thick wall or at something else which would stop the shot, just in case the worst thing happened and you loaded a live cartridge in error. If you do leave snap caps in a gun, make sure you remove them before arriving at a shoot – it is a courtesy to your fellow shooters.

STORAGE

When not in use, guns should be secured. Be careful of leaving guns in cars. If you shoot regularly, it may be worth considering some sort of secure locker in the boot. Another option is one of the new gunlips which incorporate a steel security cord that may be used both in cars and in other less-than-ideal situations away from home.

It is also common sense that guns should not be stored in conditions that are damp or subject to fluctuations or extremes of temperature (central heating can be bad for guns). If stored for long periods, guns should be taken out occasionally and inspected – pay special attention to the bores and the stock. Never use heavy grease in gun barrels, and always clean a gun very thoroughly after it has been in storage; I know of several cases where rifles have been blown up because owners have filled the bores with 'protective' grease.

Cabinets

There is a wide variety of cabinets available for storage at home, and their use is all the more important in houses where there are children.

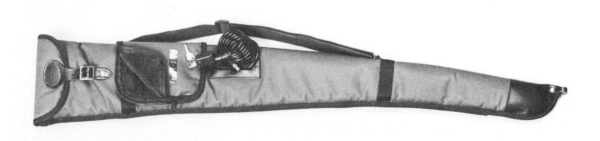

A new type of gunslip which enables you to secure a gun in the back of the car or elsewhere, when your normal gun cabinet is not available.

Never depend on others for your own or anyone else's safety. Common sense and a cool head are always important. These shooters are shooting in a flurry. Fast and furious action, and potential danger, too, as the two firing points are not separated: cross-firing is possible.

Youngsters have a special fascination for weapons, which all shooting parents should recognize and address by devoting time to satisfying the child's curiosity through proper training. Children who have been given the opportunity to examine guns, and to shoot them under proper supervision and with a strong emphasis on safety, are much less likely to handle or attempt to handle firearms when their parents are not present.

2 Sporting Disciplines

By far the most popular clay discipline in Britain is Sporting Clays, shot to English rules. Its origins are in the simulated game shooting with clay targets that the shooting schools of the great gunmakers began to offer sportsmen late in the last century. The first national championship was held in the 1920s in the suburbs of London. In those days, competitions for Sporting shooting were few; today we are spoilt for choice, as perusal of the shooting press makes clear. Two very big events in the Sporting calender are the British Open and the Game Fair shoot. Sporting competitions; as in most other sporting events, the very best shoot with the very worst, and with every level of ability in between. This is one of the great charms of Sporting shooting, and no doubt is a major factor in its continued success.

English Sporting shooting has evolved considerably in recent years. Targets have become much more challenging as more and more people have taken up this exciting pastime. One may shoot gun-up (pre-mounted) or gun-down and, typically, might shoot five pairs of targets on each stand from some sort of safety cage. Cartridges are restricted to 1oz loads and less, and pellet sizes 6–9 are permissible. Any shotgun of bore size 12 or under may be used; multichokes and guns may be changed between stands (although I would not normally suggest doing either). With repeaters, no more than two cartridges may be loaded. I shall not discuss the rules of English Sporting in any more detail here. If you want to shoot this discipline, you will need a copy of the official rule book, which is available from the Clay Pigeon Shooting Association, together with other useful publications (*see* Further Reading).

Recently, there has been a trend towards reducing the number of birds to be shot per stand in English Sporting (thus giving the shooter less opportunity to adapt to the target) and increasing the overall number of stands on many layouts. Long-range targets are much more common than they were ten years ago, although a few shots have taken long-range shooting to ridiculous extents and are in the habit of presenting silly birds which cannot be shot consistently. This damages the confidence of average shots. It is interesting to note that when top shooters turn to course design they rarely make this sort of error. They know that the best shooting course tries to beat the guns with unusual angles at middle range.

A 'round' of English Sporting might consist of anything from 20 to 100 birds shot from as many as fifteen stands. Variety is the great appeal of English Sporting. The targets are as varied as the imagination of the person who sets up the course. The general idea, though not always adhered to, is to present targets which correspond to quarry species: 'driven pheasant', 'rabbit', 'crossing pigeon', 'woodcock' or 'dropping duck'. On a typical shoot, one might encounter mini (60mm), midi (90mm), battue or rabbit clays as well as the standard (110mm) type; very occasionally, one might face the heavy rocket target. Midis are deceptively fast; minis deceptively slow. Battues are thin and fast, and turn, causing their line to change very rapidly. Rabbits and rockets can be hard to kill because they are less brittle than the other targets. Any official English Sporting shoot is limited to a maximum of 30 per cent non-standard clays.

Some Sporting targets. Left to right: battue; standard; midi; mini and rabbit. The only target not shown is the rocket.

A typical Sporting stand.

Every stand these days is likely to offer some sort of double. One might be asked to shoot at **pairs on report**, that is where the second bird is released as soon as the shooter fires at the first; or **simultaneous pairs** where both clays are launched at the same time; or **following pairs**, where the second bird is released as soon after the first as is safe and practicable, whether or not the shooter has fired at the first. Combinations of birds such as 'fur and feather' – a rabbit combined with a crosser or quartering bird – are very common. They are usually presented with second target on report, but sometimes they are launched simultaneously and become an even greater challenge. Tips for specific targets are included in Chapter 8 (*see* page 95).

REGISTERED SHOOTS

The Clay Pigeon Shooting Association maintains an averages register for classifying the performance of English Sporting shots at registered shoots – that is, competitions that are conducted to CPSA rules. Prizes at registered shoots can be very substantial, but these events are not always a good place for the less-experienced shooter to gain confidence; standards are so high now that a new shooter, even one who has been properly introduced to the sport, might have great difficulty with some of the birds. I always advise my students to start with smaller, less formal shoots. To find out where these are, you will need to buy the shooting magazines and talk with shooting friends. In some areas, you will find clay shoots advertised in the local paper. It is also likely that there is a Sporting club close to you. Visit it and, if it is safe, presents reasonable targets, and has a friendly atmosphere (the ones that do not are the exception), join it and support it. Club shooting is usually good value and a lot of fun. It is the bedrock of Sporting shooting in Britain.

The CPSA classifications for English Sporting are split into four groups: AA, A, B, and C.

Sporting shooting brings together people from all walks of life. It is good manners and fun to help out whenever possible. Here, Sheila Churchill takes her turn at scoring at the St Osyth Village gun club.

The class into which one is put depends on one's average during the previous year over a minimum of 100 targets. The 1993 figures were: class AA, 77 per cent and over; A, 69–76 per cent; B, 60–68 per cent; C, under 60 per cent. The averages book, which includes statistics for all the official disciplines, is published by the CPSA every year.

Although registered competition is undoubtedly exciting, many shooters (myself included) have doubts about the averages system as it is currently operated. Some people deliberately scheme to remain in a lower class than they ought to be, so as to improve their chances of winning class prizes. Nevertheless, for the honest competitor, annually published averages are a useful insight into performance, and a banded system of shooting classes allows shooters at all levels to enjoy competition.

UNREGISTERED ENGLISH SPORTING SHOOTS

There are many unregistered English Sporting competitions conducted every week. Like the registered shoots, they are advertised in the shooting press. Most are held on a 're-entry' basis. Sometimes a local class averages system is used; often there are special novice and lady categories. Standards of targets vary widely, from the simple birds of the local Young Farmers' shoot, to the really challenging targets of unregistered events at the top shooting

grounds like Southdown in Sussex or High Lodge in Suffolk.

In re-entry competition, the shooter may put in as many completed cards as he can afford and has time to complete. Like the averages system, this can be abused. Some re-entry shoots today are won on the fifth or sixth attempt – the winner, to a great extent, having bought his victory on the day.

Re-entry, however, allows the shooter a second bite of the cherry, and such competitions can be extremely enjoyable. Nevertheless, some of us think that it would be a good idea, and more sporting, to limit entries at these competitions to two or three cards to count. Participants could be allowed to shoot more, but only on a birds-only (practice-for-fun) basis.

The unsung heroes of Sporting shooting – the trappers.

WALK-UPS

A walk-up may be part of an English Sporting shoot, or it may be presented as a shoot on its own. A walk-up usually consists of a lane or path on either side of which traps have been concealed. It simulates a game shooter's walking up live quarry. Perhaps the most famous walk-up in the UK is the one at the West London Shooting Grounds. It always used to feature when the British Open was held at Northolt.

How does a walk-up work? The scorer explains the course (without giving too much away) and asks the shooter to load. When the shooter is ready, he is told to proceed up the path. Targets are usually released as the shooter reaches specific points, but an experienced trapper may try to catch the shooter on the wrong foot. Wonderful fun, and difficult the first time, walk-ups tend to be fairly rare because they require a large number of traps and are time consuming. They are usually shot over 20 or 25 targets, and are rarely straighted.

POOL SHOOTS

At many English Sporting competitions you will find a side event called a pool shoot. A pool shoot is usually shot over five pairs of very hard targets. A proportion of the (normally) modest entry fee goes into a kitty and the winning shooter takes a designated proportion at the end of the day. This can mount up to something quite substantial. It is rare for a pool to be won these days with less than a perfect score, and often several shooters will tie and 'shoot off' for the purse. Pool targets are usually long and awkward; but not always – sometimes they can be close and awkward! I heard of one enterprising shoot organizer who put on a special pool with mini targets presented as 'rats' scurrying down a hill and insisted on entrants' using his club's .410 to shoot them.

If you do ever find yourself in the fortunate position of getting into the final shoot-off at a pool (or indeed at any Sporting event) consider the merits of agreeing to split the prize money with your adversary and shooting off just for fun.

As well as being an excellent and challenging competition in its own right, the pool stand can also be used as a warm-up for the main shoot. However, if the pool is especially difficult, be careful that you do not break your confidence before the main event.

FLUSHES AND FLURRIES

As well as pool shoots, some major Sporting Clay competitions or country sports events will offer a 'flush' or 'flurry'. In this event a mixture of driven targets will be presented to the shooter or shooters. Occasionally set up for a single gun, flushes usually involve a team of two guns, and may be set up for a team of three or four. The organizers will, typically, be trying to catch the shooters out by putting more birds into the air than can comfortably be shot. This makes for exciting and sometimes frustrating shooting. I especially enjoy flushes where a lot of thought and planning has been put in, and where a perfect score for the team of guns is just about possible.

The keys to success at a flush are to agree a strategy if one has a partner ('You take the extreme right-handers, I'll take those on the far left') and to learn the skill of reloading as quickly as possible. As soon as you have fired your second shot – usually you will not be able to load more than two cartridges, even if you have a gun with greater capacity – reload immediately. Fumble-free loading will be made much easier if you have cartridges in easy reach, rim up. It is worth spending a little time one day practising for these situations. One of the few disadvantages of over-and-under guns is made clear in flushes: many of them do not open that wide, and may be marginally slower to reload than an equivalent side-by-side.

The two-man flush.

SUPER SPORTING

Super Sporting is a variation of English Sporting. It has been developed by shooting instructor and former World FITASC Champion, John Bidwell, at his Suffolk shooting ground, High Lodge. Super Sporting is usually a 100-bird shoot. At each stand, ten targets will be shot, with three traps in action. It is a little like FITASC shooting (*see* page 35) although a gundown rule is not enforced. A typical Super Sporting stand might include a rabbit, a tower bird and a quartering target from a trap positioned quite close to the shooting cage. John has two ways of setting his Super Sporting stands up. One involves starting with three singles, one from each trap (full use of gun), then three report pairs. The final bird is another single. The other way he presents his targets is as five pairs. In either case, the first bird of each pair remains constant so that the shooter does not become confused. Super Sporting offers a little more target variation than traditional English Sporting. Like FITASC, it requires a clear head.

SPORTING CLAYS: AMERICAN RULES

Sporting has taken off in a big way in the States. An embryonic version was introduced by the Remington Arms company some time ago, and then it was reintroduced and popularized there by the Orvis Company in the 1980s. The main organization involved in regulating Sporting Clays in the United States is the National Sporting Clays Association, a division of the National Skeet Shooting Association, (*see* Useful Addresses).

The American version of Sporting Clays is similar to English Sporting in many ways; but there are important differences too. A 'gun-down' rule is enforced in the US (specifically, the heel of the butt must be positioned below the armpit until the target is seen). In American Sporting 1⅛oz loads may still be used. There are other differences, but they do not apply to all shoots: there can be up to a three-second delay on calling 'Pull!'; occasionally there are 'poisoned species' – of a different colour to standard clays – which must not be shot (this is seen in the UK, too, where the no-shoot birds tend to be called 'protected species'); another variation sometimes seen in the US is 'timed reloading', which involves setting a maximum allowable time for reloading on a particular stand. Finally, it is worth noting that many grounds in the US now insist that shooters wear both ear and eye protection.

FITASC SPORTING

In FITASC Sporting (*Fédération Internationale de Tir aux Armes Sportives de Chasse*), which is typically more challenging than English (or American) Sporting, there is a far greater variety of targets. It was designed by the French and formalized in the 1960s. Typically, at each FITASC stand, one might engage targets from four or five different automatic traps, although there may be more. The typical FITASC shoot might be 150 birds over six different layouts (FITASC is always shot in multiples of 25). Major championships usually consist of 200 birds shot over several days.

On each FITASC layout (a mini Sporting shoot in itself) there are a number of stands or 'posts' (four are typical), and at each one the shooter is required to shoot at single and

Barry Simpson, one of the best FITASC shooters in the world. (Photograph by courtesy of Gunmark Ltd.)

double targets. The singles are shot first, then the doubles, which must be combinations of the various singles thrown.

Waiting to shoot does not usually pose a problem in FITASC Sporting, as it can in English Sporting, because FITASC is a 'squadded' discipline. This means that one must shoot every stand on the layout with the same pre-arranged small group of people. However, one disadvantage to FITASC is that although there is little waiting while out shooting, there is considerable delay between squads. With English Sporting the shooter can, with luck, be finished in an hour or two. This is never the case with FITASC; usually it takes a whole day and, for the big competitions, two days.

The variation of targets in FITASC is greater than in English Sporting, and one has far less chance to adapt to the angle of the birds; one may not watch other squads in action.

Cartridges can be loaded with up to $1\frac{1}{4}$oz of shot and, for singles, one has 'full use of gun' (meaning two shots may be fired). All FITASC shooters must adopt a 'gun-down' position. According to the rule book (FITASC Sporting Rules: Rule 1.05):

The shooter will adopt a ready position . . . with the heel of the gun touching the body under a horizontal line marked on the shooter's jacket. This line will be indicated by a tape of contrasting colour fixed to the jacket by some semi-permanent means. The horizontal line shall be located 25cm below an imaginary line drawn along the top of the shoulders along their axis.

Another stipulation of FITASC shooting is that one may not raise the gun or move the muzzles until the target or targets are in sight, nor may one pre-mount the gun. This is sensible, and no disadvantage whatsoever to a good shot: mounting the gun early may be considered a fault in technique. There are no safety cages in FITASC and safe gun handling is of paramount importance: it is certainly not a discipline for

novice shooters. One of the nice things about FITASC is that it is usually very carefully and fairly refereed.

FITASC is a wonderfully challenging sport, probably the best all-round test of shooting ability available to clay shooters. The only disadvantage is that it is more expensive than English Sporting and, because of the requirement to organize squads, it must usually be booked in advance. As with English Sporting, the CPSA run a class system. The 1993 figures were: A, 74 per cent and over; B, 65–73 per cent; C, under 65 per cent. There are only three classes. Shoot-offs in FITASC are usually settled over 25 birds.

PRO TRAP

The essence of Pro Trap, an unofficial discipline, is that there is a single firing point from which the shooter engages a wide variety of fairly demanding Sporting-type targets from half a dozen or more traps. I have seen two versions of Pro Trap. One involves the shooter's engaging predesignated targets; the other presents the shooter with targets in random order, but with the qualification that all shooters will shoot the same set of birds by the time they have finished their round. A round of Pro Trap is usually 25 birds.

Sometimes Pro Trap target release is computer controlled (but a similar result may be achieved by giving the buttoner a set of cards corresponding to the various targets on offer, and shuffling them between shooters. I have never seen a gun-down rule enforced at Pro Trap.

PRO SPORTING

Another new, and as yet unofficial, discipline which, like Pro Trap, combines some of the advantages of both English Sporting and FITASC, is Pro Sporting as developed by Ian

Cawthorne and Ray Hulston at the South West Shooting School in North Devon (and by others in slightly different form).

In Pro Sporting, there are four or five traps set up in front of five stands or plates – similar to those on a Trap shooting layout. There is also a waiting position behind each shooting position, so there is no danger of a shooter swinging down the line when engaging tightly angled targets. The key concept is that a line of five shooters is presented with a wide combination of fairly hard targets without having to walk around a Sporting layout in the normal way.

It works out something like this: the shooter, who may adopt a gun-up or gun-down position as in English Sporting, will occupy one of the stands where, on calling 'Pull!', a predesignated pair of targets will be released either on report or simultaneously. Having shot the first pair, the shooter then calls for a second pair of predesignated targets, clears the gun and falls back to the waiting position, relaxing while the other participants take their turn at the targets designated for their particular position. When everyone has shot, each moves along one position.

Everything happens quite quickly and most who have tried this form of shooting find it rather more exciting than traditional Sporting shooting because you are in immediate competition with the shooters next to you. Shooting continues over ten pairs (i.e. a normal round is 20 rather than 25 birds), but for the second half of the round, the combination offered on each stand will change. In other words, everyone will shoot from the same position twice, but the target combinations will be different.

As with FITASC, there are no safety cages, so safe gun handling is vital. One may load only on the firing point and, as on a Trap Shooting line, the gun is closed only when it is your turn to shoot. Pro Sporting is excellent sport, as testing as FITASC, and is cheaper and far quicker to shoot.

BIRDBRAIN

This is a computer-controlled shoot (the computer unit which controls target release is called a 'Birdbrain'), which is similar to Pro Sporting (although it predates it). Typically, Birdbrain uses seven traps. Popularized in the UK by former Olympic Skeet shooter, Paul Bentley, Birdbrain is organized much like a Trap shoot. There are five firing points (but each has its own cage), from which one fires at five targets before moving on. The targets to be engaged are Sporting in character and before shooting, the participant does not know what will be presented, except that it may be a single (full use of gun) or a double. Gun start position is up to the individual. The technique for this sort of shoot is considered in the section on unpredictable targets in Chapter 8 (*see* page 102).

AMERICAN FIVE STAND

Five Stand is a very similar game to Pro Sporting and Birdbrain. There are five safety cages – positioned anything between three and seven yards (2.5 and 6.5m) apart – and anything between six and eight automatic traps may be used. According to the NSCA, who regulate the discipline, shooting 'will take place in squads of five or less and each shooter will shoot a round of 25 targets on each layout. Shooting will commence with the shooter on stand 1 calling for a target.' Targets may all be singles or a mixture of singles and simultaneous doubles. Five Stand shooters must adopt a gun-down position, 'the stock must be visible under the armpit'. After shooting at a single (full use of gun) or double, the next position shoots, and so on. When each shooter has shot a total of five targets from the same position, everyone moves on to the next cage. A version of Five Stand is currently being promoted in the UK under the name 'Compak Sporting' by the Laporte company; it has just been accepted by FITASC as an official discipline. It utilizes a

The Birdbrain computer. (Photograph by courtesy of Guns and Shooting.*)*

The new discipline of Compak Sporting.

four-cage firing point and a minimum of six traps is stipulated, including a rabbit and a teal. It is clear that disciplines like Pro Sporting, Five Stand and Compak are going to grow. They offer great Sporting shooting in limited space.

'SNOOKER'

Snooker, the invention of Richard Ford, chief instructor at the Parkford Shooting Centre, Saint Osyth, Essex, is a fun shoot which may also be used as a pool shoot. Snooker is a variation on Pro Trap, but the shooter collects points corresponding to the designated value of the targets he hits rather than merely gaining one point for one kill as normal. The game borrows its scoring concept (more or less) from the game of snooker. One must shoot a red 'ball' to start, which will always be an easy target (scoring 1 point), then one may go for any colour: yellow (2 points), green (3 points), brown (4 points), blue (5 points), pink (6 points) or black (7 points). The targets are progressively more difficult according to this colour coding. If the shooter kills the coloured bird, he must kill another red before moving on to another colour. Once the individual has shot five reds and five colours, the colours must be shot in order as in a snooker 'break'. Missing any target means handing over the firing point to the next shooter. There is a second way of playing the game whereby the shooter may continue after a miss, and shoots at five reds and the colours: maximum possible break, 32.

SIMULATED GAME

These shoots are similar to flushes, and involve lots of driven targets coming towards a line of shooters. Typically, they simulate a day on driven pheasant or partridge, although one might have a simulated grouse shoot or, indeed, anything else which takes the organizer's fancy. Some organizers are now using computer-controlled traps, which ensure that each 'peg' gets a very similar set of birds. The best simulated shoots are very similar to a formal game shoot in all respects but one: you cannot eat the targets you shoot! I have had a lot of fun on such days, but note that some organizers are not as careful about safety as they should be. I think it is a potentially dangerous practice to have a staggered line on a simulated game day (a line where there is a front and rear line of guns). A safety briefing by the shoot captain is essential before proceedings commence, because such days bring together different ability levels and shooters with different experiences, notably clay shooters and driven game shooters.

CRAZY QUAIL

An American invention, Crazy Quail uses a rotating trap in a pit. The trap can move a full 360 degrees, and the shooters stand anywhere from sixteen to twenty yards in front of the pit. To quote US writer Art Blatt, 'The target may be delayed up to ten seconds after a competitor calls "Pull!" . . . The shooter may not, for safety reasons, turn and fire at an incoming target after it passes him.' A handicap-by-distance system is sometimes used at Crazy Quail, but it is essentially a fun shoot without formal rules.

DUCK TOWER

The American version of a traditional English high tower, but instead of simulating driven pheasants, the duck tower simulates the sort of shot one gets from a hide when shooting wildfowl in the United States.

STAR SHOT

Invented by Scottish clay shooter David Maxwell, Star Shot involves a large metal frame

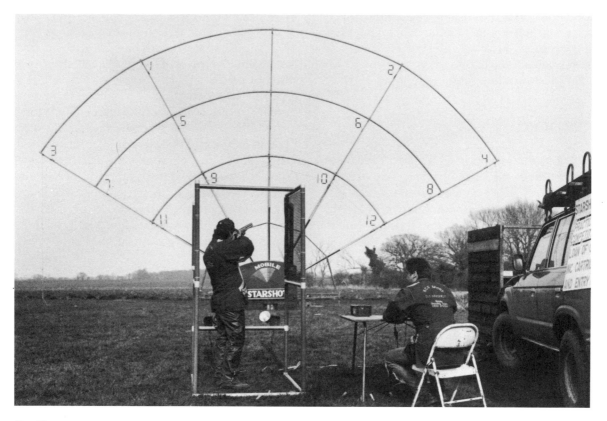

Star Shot.

placed in front of four traps which present the shooter with steeply rising targets at various angles. The challenge is to break the target within a certain segment of the frame.

Star Shot was designed specifically to make clay shooting a television sport, and pro-celebrity matches have been broadcast both in the UK and in the United States. It is a rather artificial and very quick discipline, but fun. Because of the nature of some of the targets it presents, it can be a good means to learn how to shoot targets by maintained lead and interception. The latter is not a technique I would advise for most Sporting shooting, but the advanced competitor needs to know how to employ it, and Star Shot is an enjoyable means to this end apart from being fun in its own right.

SKEET

Skeet, on the other hand, is excellent Sporting practice. Indeed, it might be argued that Skeet is actually the first Sporting discipline. It was invented by two keen American game shooters – William Foster and C.E. Davis – around 1915. They were looking for a means of off-season practice which tested their shooting at as many angles as possible and, according to legend, enabled them to prove who was the best shot.

Initially, Foster and Davis' game involved a single trap and a full circle with inward facing shooting positions at each 'hour'. To eliminate the problem of a 360-degree safety zone (and complaints from neighbours), they modified this set-up. Instead of a single trap and a circle,

Skeet shooting is a great way to improve your Sporting shooting, and a wonderful discipline in its own right.

they had two traps facing each other at opposite ends of a semicircle, with one trap higher than the other. It became Skeet in 1926, when an American Sporting magazine offered a $100 prize for creating a name for the new sport, which until then was called 'Shooting Round the Clock'. A housewife called Gertrude Hurlbutt won with 'Skeet' – a Scandinavian name for shooting (and also, I recently discovered, an Afrikaans word for our sport).

Skeet involves mainly crossing and quartering targets at moderate to close ranges, and is shot to a variety of different rules today. In Olympic Skeet (formerly ISU Skeet), the competitor must shoot from an exaggerated gun-down position, with the butt of the gun touching the hip bone, and with a random delay of up to three seconds after calling for the target. The targets in Olympic Skeet are very fast, and it is, without doubt, the most difficult of the Skeet disciplines. An admirable, but specialist sport, Olympic Skeet is not particularly popular in Great Britain or the USA (in both countries the domestic Skeet disciplines predominate).

In American and English Skeet, a gun-up position is legal, but not necessarily advantageous, and the birds are slower (English birds are very slightly slower than American NSSA regulation targets, but both are considerably slower than Olympic targets). The principle difference between English and American Skeet (which itself is becoming increasingly popular in the UK, especially in East Anglia around the US airbases) is that in English Skeet

41

Olympic Skeet. Note the low position of the gun butt.

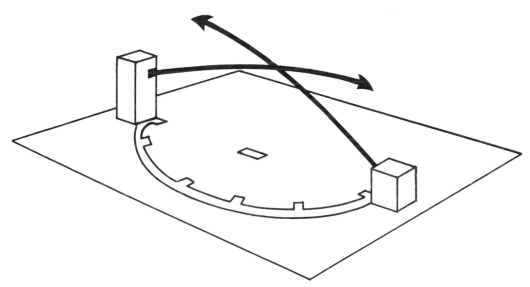

A Skeet shooting layout. English Skeet does not use the position in the middle – Station 8.

the competitor must shoot a double on Stand 4, but does not have to shoot from Station 8. Station 8 is situated midway between the high and low houses. In NSSA skeet one faces a driven single from each house at this station. Many American Skeet shooters compete with tubed guns in special events which involve the 12, 20, 28 and .410 (these tubes reduce the bore size of a normal 12-bore so that smaller-bore cartridges may safely be fired from a

single gun). The Americans also have an interesting Skeet game called Doubles which, as the name implies, involves shooting at pairs of targets.

All Skeet ranges are set up as shown in the diagram on page 42, but the sequence in which birds are shot, and the distance they are thrown, varies.

Skeet is a wonderful technique builder for Sporting shooting, particularly when it is practised from a gun-down position. To get perfect scores in Skeet – and few competitions are won these days with anything less than a perfect score – requires the greatest mental discipline. One must also be in the habit of changing one's foot and gun-point positions between stands – a vital skill for the Sporting shooter to acquire.

The scores of top Skeet shooters are quite phenomenal – shoot-offs running into hundreds of birds without a miss are not unknown. According to the CPSA class system, in 1993 an average of 93 per cent or more the year before was needed to shoot in AA; 88–92 per cent for A; 80–87 per cent for B; and under 80 per cent for C. It is very rare for a score of less than 98 to win a competition, and hundred-straights are common. Because Skeet is such excellent practice for Sporting, I have included some specific Skeet shooting tips in Chapter 8, (*see* page 104).

TRAP

You may be surprised to see Trap shooting mentioned here, but it is eminently worth considering in a book orientated towards Sporting Clays because, like Skeet, it can offer excellent practice for Sporting.

The Trap shooting disciplines – Down-the-Line (DTL), Automatic Ball Trap (ABT), Olympic Trap (OT), Universal Trench (UT), etc. – have all evolved from live pigeon shooting, which was very popular in the last century and is still practised in Spain, Portugal and Mexico. All Trap shooting involves engaging

Shooting Down-the-Line (DTL). The clay is about to break and you can see the shot charge halfway between it and the muzzles.

retreating targets at rather long ranges with a trap set up well in front of the shooter (16 yards (15m) at DTL). If you really want to improve your Sporting shooting try DTL from a gun-down position. All the Trap shooting disciplines not only offer useful long-range quartering targets for Sporting practice but, as an activity in their own right, they are a first-class means for the Sporting shooter to develop mental discipline.

3 Gun Choice

Many different opinions have been expressed as to the ideal gun for Sporting shooting. Twenty years ago, many good shots used an open-bored, short-barrelled Skeet gun for close targets and a tight-bored, long-barrelled Trap gun for long targets; some even used a game gun as well for the targets in between. Then the age of the multichoke arrived and people started to become neurotic choke changers, instead of neurotic gun changers!

My own philosophy is to keep everything as simple as possible. I use the same 31½in-barrelled over-and-under for all the English disciplines (Sporting Skeet and DTL) and feel at no great disadvantage. I like the stability and pointability of a long, fairly heavy gun. It soaks up the recoil, reduces blast effect, and promotes follow-through too. Moreover, the perception of lead seems to be different with the long gun; the illusion is that it requires less lead.

Although I use a long-barrelled gun myself, my experience as a shooting instructor leads me to advise most students of normal build to begin their Sporting shooting career with a 30in gun of medium weight – about 8lbs – although for anyone under 5ft 6in, I should probably advise a 28in). I am firmly against very light guns for clay shooting because they recoil more and require a more conscious approach to follow-through. 30s and 28s may not

Conventional multichokes.

Two improved multichoke changing keys.

be quite so pointable as the 30in-plus guns, but they are easier to learn to use because they handle more instinctively. The long guns require a more deliberate approach which seems to suit experienced shooters better. The time to change to one (if ever) is only after several seasons of shooting, by which time you should have developed the control necessary to use one properly.

I have Nigel Teague's Precision Chokes (precision multichokes) in my competition Sporter but I never change them. I use ½ and tight ½ for everything: my attention is never distracted by worrying about what chokes to use. I know ½ and ½ will kill any target (¼ and ¼ probably will as well – but ½ and ½ also allows me to see *where* I am hitting the bird). Even though I do not change my own chokes, I usually advise my students to buy a multi-choked gun because it allows one to shoot with open chokes in the early stages of one's shooting

Long choke tubes by Nigel Teague. They have a very gentle taper, which is said to improve pattern quality by reducing pellet disruption and deformation. (Photograph by courtesy of Nigel Teague.)

over-and-under is king on the Sporting Clays field. It has an uncluttered sighting plane, and controls recoil more effectively than the traditional side-by-side gun. Among my own favourite guns are the Browning B25s and 125s, the Beretta 682s (and the old 680s), and the Perazzi MX8. The Browning 325s and the 686 and 687 Berettas offer good value for money, as do nearly all Miroku guns. I especially like the Miroku 6000 fixed-choke Sporter.

Krieghoff guns modelled on the old Remington 32 are excellent, but expensive to buy new. Winchesters based on the 101-type action are excellent guns and, in the UK at least, a good second-hand buy. Other useful guns include the Ruger Red Label, especially the Sporting Clays model with back-bored, long cones and 30in barrels, the new Remington Peerless, and the Sporters made by Laurona

career. Moreover, because multichoke guns are currently in fashion, they are easier to sell.

There has been quite a lot of talk recently about the new, longer, multichokes. Browning now provide them as standard on their guns, and Nigel Teague offers his long chokes as a retrofit option. Briley, in the United States, has offered long chokes for some time. I think long chokes and long forcing cones make sense. The idea behind them is that they decrease pellet deformation and reduce disturbance to the wad and shot as they travel down the barrel. We shall consider chokes and forcing cones in more detail later (*see* pages 141–3 and 149–50), but for now, let me make the point that if you do opt for a multichoke gun, pattern it with each of the choke tubes provided – often you will find that the patterns do not correspond to the marked chokings.

ACTION TYPE AND BARREL FORMAT

What type of gun is best – over-and-under, side-by-side or semi-auto? Undoubtedly, the

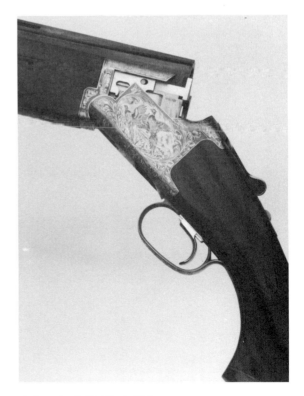

A Browning B325 Grade V Sporter.

47

A Beretta 687 Sporter. (Photograph by courtesy of Gunmark Ltd.)

and and Lanber. Finally, I might mention that Holland and Holland have recently launched a new range of over-and-unders, including a true sidelock and a gun with a detachable trigger unit like a Perazzi. Both shoot extremely well, but they are expensive.

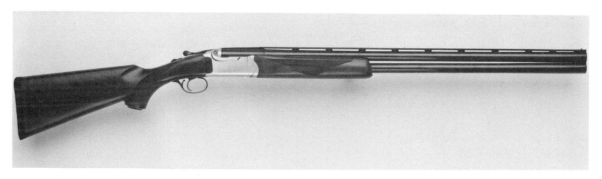

The Ruger Sporting Clays model. It combines back-bored barrels and long forcing cones as standard features. (Photograph by courtesy of Sturm Ruger and Co.)

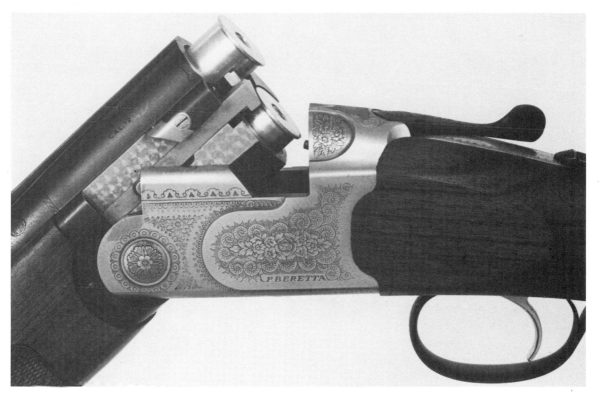

The action of a 686 Beretta Sporter. Note the snap caps. I am a little wary of using these regularly because of the potential confusion with live cartridges. (Photograph by courtesy of Gunmark Ltd.)

Although, over-and-unders are my first choice for Sporting shooting, semi-autos are very good value, and can be used very effectively on Sporting Clays (one of the very few 100-straights at Sporting was achieved with a semi-auto – a Remington 1100). Apart from modest cost, the principle advantage of the semi-auto, if of the gas-operated type, is its light recoil. Brian Hebditch uses a gas-operated semi-auto very effectively, as does top Sporting shot Duncan Lawton. Dan Carlisle, the great American Trap and Skeet competitor, who has now turned his attention to Sporting shooting, is another who prefers this type of weapon. Recoil-operated semi-autos are not usually very effective tools for Sporting, although they can be used with deadly effect against live game.

Of the gas guns, I would recommend the old Remington 1100 and, especially, their new 11-87 'Light Contour' model. I have recently tested one of these extensively and found it comfortable to shoot, well balanced and utterly reliable. Apart from a new lightweight barrel, the gun has the ingeniously simple 11-87 self-metering gas regulator which ensures that almost any cartridge may be used without problem. The Beretta 300 series guns are also very good; they have an alloy action and are a bit lighter than Remingtons. Gas-operated semi-autos, especially in 20-bore, are the perfect choice for lightly built, recoil-shy novices: many shooting schools keep such a 20-bore auto for teaching young people.

What about side-by-sides? I love a good side-by-side and often use one for game shooting,

The detachable trigger group – a feature on many Perazzi guns. It comes out of the action body by pushing the safety catch forward beyond its normal position. Perazzi guns also have easily detachable stocks.

The Remington 1100: one of the best ever semi-automatic designs. The updated 11-87 version has a self-metering gas system which makes it even better.

but it is, in my opinion, essentially a tool for instinctive shooting. There is no doubt that the side-by-side can be used effectively against Sporting Clay targets (look what Percy Stanbury did with one), and it is great fun to make one work, but it is not the tool of choice today. Side-by-sides are rarely available with reliable single trigger mechanisms; they have a tendency to 'flip' down in the first phase of recoil, and they are usually made too light to absorb recoil effectively. All this said, there are some side-by-sides that are more suitable for Sporting shooting than others: the Beretta 626, the new AyA Model 722, the old Winchester 23, the Japanese-made Winchester 21, and some of the old Webley guns designed for Trap or live pigeon shooting. Any long-barrelled pigeon or wildfowling side-by-side with a flat top rib and a pistol or semi-pistol grip, might be converted into a useful Sporter by removing some of the choke or having it multichoked.

What about pump guns? Theoretically a pump gun could be used effectively at Sporting (on occasion, I take out an old Winchester Model 1897 just for fun). However, I have yet to see a pump gun used successfully in Sporting competition. Semiconscious though it may have become to the experienced user, the trombone action required of the left hand is a handicap to most of us, at least those not brought up with the pump. Nevertheless, there is absolutely no reason why the owner of a pump gun should not use it to have a go at Sporting. Pumps have been used with the greatest success at Skeet and Trap in the United States, and are the weapon of choice of many American hunters. The Winchester Model 12 is probably the best pump gun ever made, but the Remington 870 is an excellent gun too, with a very smooth cycle thanks to its twin-action bars.

SMALL-BORES

Twenty-bore over-and-unders are currently quite popular on the Sporting field. Some are wonderfully elegant little guns but, as far as serious competition is concerned, they are a handicap. Some might dispute this; there are a few gifted shots who use 20-bores at Sporting and beat the 12s – men like Andrew Perkins of the Holland & Holland Shooting School – but to produce really good scores requires a lot of hard work because the margin for error with a 20-bore is less. Thirty-inch-barrelled 20-bores have become popular with game shooters recently, and are probably the most effective of the 20-bores at Sporting as well. If you are an experienced shot, and intent on a twenty (and they are undeniably a lot of fun to use) you would be well advised to go for the longer barrel length.

The diminutive 28-bore and .410 are not really a practical proposition for Sporting competition, though they can be useful for teaching the very young; of the two, the 28 is a much better gun.

RIBS

A clay shooting gun should have some sort of rib. However, it should be understood that when shooting, the rib should be seen in one's peripheral vision only: it is an aid to consistent gun mounting. For those who have not yet discovered a preference, I recommend a flat 10mm (middle width) rib. Steeply ramped or stepped ribs should be avoided for Sporting shooting, since they can disturb perception of the target because the eye is distracted by an irregular sighting plane.

Tapered ribs have become a bit of a fad in recent years. I like a slight taper – it looks better proportioned to my eye – but I cannot honestly say that a tapered rib makes much difference to my shooting, though the suggestion that a tapered rib draws the eye to the target makes some sense. One of the best ribs I have ever seen is on the Perazzi MX8 DG2; it combines a slight taper, a subtle ramp and a shallow $\frac{1}{10}$in

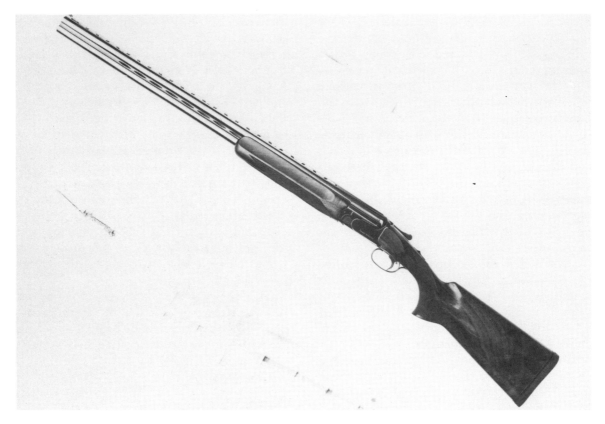

A Perazzi MX8DG2 – one of my own favourite competition guns.

(2mm) wide centre channel. Although I do not favour them, some shooters like wide ribs. It is sometimes said that a wider rib effectively creates a bit of built-in lead on the gun for crossing targets, and I am willing to give them the benefit of the doubt. The super-wide-ribbed guns were once very popular in both Skeet and Trap shooting.

Finally, there are two qualities (applicable to all designs) that are always worth looking for in a rib: it should be absolutely true, and finished with some sort of effective non-reflective surface; if a rib is deficient in either of these respects it will distract the eye and take focus off the target. On a gun that is otherwise satisfactory, it may be worth modifying or even changing the rib. Such work is expensive, however.

STOCKS

Stocks are a very personal thing, and opinions vary regarding what is and what is not comfortable almost as much as individual technique and physique do. I might note that many people's guns do not fit them, and moreover, many are saddled not just with ill-fitting stocks, but with poorly deisgned ones (for which manufacturers must take the blame). Some 'Sporters' are often no more than dressed up Trap guns; others cannot so easily be categorized, but are poorly suited to the purpose for which they are sold.

A real Sporter is something of a compromise. It should be designed to point well, but also be stable to swing. Its stock should have been

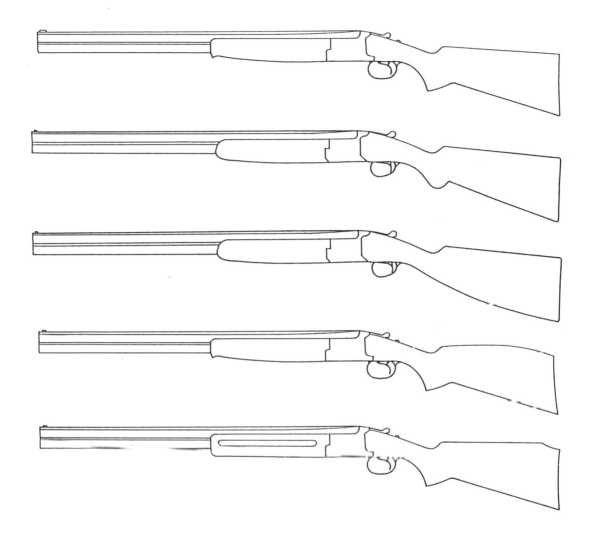

Different stock configurations for Sporting guns. The top gun is very typical, with full pistol grip and Schnabel fore-end. The next gun has a half-pistol stock, which I think is ideal for Sporting Shooting because it promotes a very comfortable hand position. The third gun has the swan-neck stock seen on some Brownings. The fourth stock has a butt that is parallel forward of the point of facial contact; such designs are worth serious consideration by gunmakers. The bottom gun is a Trap type with a comb that has been lowered for Sporting use; I call this shape a 'semi-Monte Carlo'.

designed so that the muzzles may be controlled well with the gun out of the shoulder (which requires the right combination of grip and fore-end). A good Sporter stock will glide into position under the cheek bone, will positively locate there, and will be shaped so as to keep recoil to a minimum. Generally speaking, I think many combs are too thick, and many grips badly shaped. I much prefer the traditional shape of the English stock to the bulbous Trap type seen on some so called 'Sporters'. The tapered English comb relieves the face in recoil and prevents mismounting. The ideal stock-comb would copy the profile of a Purdey Pigeon gun, which is a little thicker than the classic game gun stock but incorporates a beautiful taper and comb profile. It is also good design practice to keep the slope on the comb to a minimum. A gun that has too much drop 'at heel' (the rear of the comb) and too little 'at comb' (the front of the comb) will recoil more than it needs to.

Shooters with long necks may find it worth considering a higher combed Monte Carlo stock (the Monte Carlo step need not be exaggerated), so they can achieve the right eye-to-rib relationship and comfortable positioning at the shoulder. A good stocker will be able to modify your gun to almost any specification you want: thick combs may be thinned, wood may even be inlet into the stock to create a Monte Carlo comb without buying a new gun. Time and money spent in refining gunfit are well spent.

What grip shape is best? This is very much a question of personal taste too. Most agree that the traditional, narrow, straight-hand stock of the classic English side-by-side is not very suitable for Sporting. For Sporting targets, a sensibly proportioned full or semi-pistol grip is the handle of choice because it affords maximum muzzle control. When buying a gun, or modifying it, I look for a grip shape that will allow my hand to fall into a natural and comfortable position on the stock. Anything which forces me to cock my wrist up or down is going to create tension. A very full pistol grip, though it might suit a Trap gun, can impede the shooter's swing. Such grips are designed for pulling the gun back into the shoulder, rather than pushing it out towards the target as is good form in Sporting shooting.

Another feature I look for in a grip is reasonably consistent depth. A grip that is very deep at the rear but shallow at the front – as the grips on many Continental guns originally designed for Trap shooting tend to be – can slip out of the hand in recoil. Generally, the grips on tra-

ditionally made guns seem much better conceived than those on today's mass-produced products (though Browning and Miroku guns are exceptions, with an excellent standard grip shape on most of their Sporters).

A further point which some manufacturers seem to forget is that grip and fore-end design should complement one another. For example, it is undesirable to have a very wide, deep, fore-end on a gun with a thin straight grip, or a very shallow, narrow, fore-end on a gun which has an oversize grip. Grip and fore-end should encourage both hands to work together. My own preference is for a semi-pistol grip of medium thickness, combined with a parallel-sided and not too deep fore-end. Semi-pistol grips are not seen on many over-and-unders these days, but any good stocker will be able to convert a full pistol grip into a semi-pistol type.

Palm swells are another feature that most Sporting guns would do better without. In principle, palm swells – a form of ergonomically shaped grip to fit the hollow formed in the palm when the hand is gripping – seem a good idea; but in practice there is too much variation between shooters' hands and it is a matter of luck whether a palm swell fits or not – most do not. If you have a palm swell which is uncomfortable, any competent stocker can remove it.

SIDELOCK OR BOXLOCK?

If you can afford a beautiful hand-built sidelock, by all means spend your money. Sidelocks, typically, have better trigger pulls, and more space for engraving. Some also argue they are better balanced – they put more weight between the hands – but on this point I have my doubts (*see* the section on balance on page 140).

I am fond of sidelocks; apart from the sophistication of their mechanism they can be works of art, but far more competitions are won with the boxlocks. No gun is more reliable than a

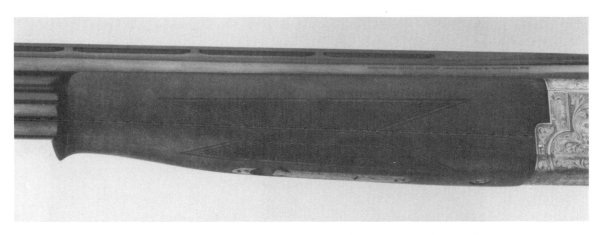

The Schnabel-type fore-end which many Sporting shooters prefer. My own preference, however, is for a parallel-sided, Trap-type fore-end, as long as it is not too wide or too deep.

A side-by-side sidelock made for John Rigby & Co. Side-by-sides are fun to shoot, but they do not win the prizes in big Sporting competitions. (Photograph by courtesy of Paul Roberts.)

good, machine-made, but hand-finished box-lock over-and-under.

Having noted my prejudice in favour of boxlock over-and-unders for Sporting Clays, it is worth noting now that some are much better than others. As with most things in life, you tend to get what you pay for. I never advise shooters to buy cheap guns. The best-value guns are in the middle price bracket. It is difficult to go far wrong with a standard gun by Browning, Miroku or Beretta. They offer excellent value for money, hold their value well (because they last well), and are backed up by first-rate service facilities. I also have a special fondness for the old Winchesters.

TRAP GUNS

Many Sporting shooters use Trap guns for Sporting. Typically, Trap guns are heavy, have long barrels, lots of choke and high combs. Quite a few top shots have used Trap guns as the basis of their Sporters. 'Sporterizing' a Trap gun may involve nothing more than reducing the comb height a bit (Trap guns usually leave the factory designed to shoot a bit high because Trap targets tend to be rising). Another common modification is to replace the fixed chokes with multichokes. The advantage to a Trap gun converted in this way is that the barrels are often a bit lighter than a 32in gun with factory multichokes. A 32in fixed-choke Miroku converted in this way is a superb and economical Sporter; 32in fixed-choke Beretta 682s respond well to the treatment too. Most of my Sporting guns started life as fixed-choke Trap guns.

ESSENCE OF A GOOD GUN

Are there any special characteristics to look for in a gun? Ideally, I think an over-and-under should have as low a profile as possible; such designs not only look more elegant but are less prone to vibration and muzzle flip and seem to

flow with the hands and eye better. Good trigger pulls are also essential (I can manage to shoot most guns, but I really dislike shooting a gun with poor trigger pulls because I find they disrupt my timing). Poor balance also distracts me. Most of my guns are set up so that they will balance on, or just ahead of, the hinge-pin. A well-balanced heavy gun seems lighter than a poorly balanced gun of lighter weight. Balance modifications are considered on page 140 in more detail.

BUYING SECOND-HAND

Most modern guns have an indefinite life expectancy if they are well cared for: if the buyer exercises care, there are many second-hand bargains to be found. A mid-range gun in as-new condition may be bought for 25–30 per cent less than its new retail price; in more worn but serviceable condition, it might be possible to buy it privately for 50–60 per cent of the new price, sometimes less. The bargains seem to get better at the top end of the market, so much so that I would rarely advise anyone to buy any 'Deluxe' model new.

It really pays to shop around for any gun these days. New or second-hand, the differences between different dealers' prices for the same product can be substantial. That said, it is also important to develop a relationship with your gun shop; this will help you out of all sorts of problems. There are still a few shops that combine old-fashioned personal service with very competitive prices. Find one.

I have already considered gun condition in some detail in Chapter 1 (*see* pages 22–3), but another very important consideration when buying second-hand, or indeed new, is gunfit. If you are buying a gun, go to an established firm and, having selected a model, ask them to check the fit. They will be unable to do this definitively in the shop – but they can at least make sure you are not buying a gun that is grossly misfitting.

Gunfit

Here are two simple, but very approximate tests for gunfit. (More information on this topic can be found in Chapter 10.)

For Length

1.   Prove the gun empty.

2.   Hold the grip normally and place the finger on the trigger (the trigger should make contact in the area between the pad and the first joint).

3.   See if the butt reaches the crook of the arm. A gun that is too short will not reach; a gun that is too long will cause you to open out the elbow joint to accommodate it. Note, however, that this is only a rough guide and is most suited to checking stock length for inexperienced shots.

For Drop and Cast

1.   Prove the gun empty.

2.   Select a point just above head height on a solid wall.

3.   Keep focusing on that point and mount the gun.

4.   Focus on the spot again, but this time, as you bring the gun up, close your eyes.

5.   Open your eyes. If you see too much or too little rib, or if you are coming up to one side or the other of the rib, *and your mounting technique is sound*, it is likely that the gun does not fit.

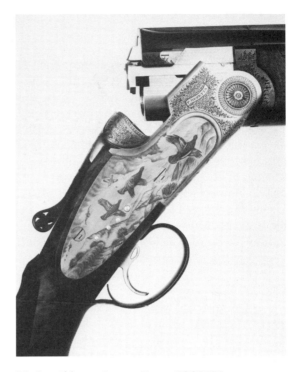

The beautiful engraving on a Beretta SO3EELL: a joy to behold but no passport to competition success. (Photograph by courtesy of Gunmark Ltd.)

CONCLUSIONS

If you are planning to buy a gun, try out as many models as you can first. Usually, people at clubs are more than willing to let you try their gun. Once you have bought a gun, however, stick with it. If you already have a gun, and you have performed reasonably well with it, do not be easily tempted to spend money on something new; you will probably be better off spending your funds on having your existing gun properly fitted, or if this is not needed, on extra shooting or instruction. Just because a gun has lovely wood and beautiful engraving does not mean it is going to shoot any better. I will end on a piece of advice that I wish I had heeded: if you ever have the good fortune to acquire a gun which seems exactly right, never part with it.

CLOTHING AND ACCESSORIES

Clothing is important to good shooting. It should offer protection from the weather without impeding body movement. There are many good shooting vests on the market; finding a good waterproof is much harder. Ideally, the shooter wants something which is very thin, so that gun mounting is only minimally affected by it.

The new generation of breathable, plastic fabrics like Gore-tex are ideal for wet-weather shooting suits, even though they are rather expensive. Be especially careful when you buy a waterproof. The arm movement, cuffs and pockets must be just right, otherwise you will be wasting your money. When shooting in really cold weather, I trust to layers rather than bulk. I always prefer to wear a vest (or vests) and a medium or thin sweater rather than relying on a thick sweater which can impede gun mounting and alter gunfit. Whenever you are buying clothes for shooting, take your gun along, or at least borrow one in the shop.

Shoes

Shoes are important. I prefer a shoe that can be used in any conditions. The ideal shooting shoe will have a rubber sole and a traditional heel. Some like to shoot in trainers, but I find that

All Sporting shooters will require wet-weather gear. Buy whatever is comfortable for you, but be careful that your arm movement is not restricted. Note that one shooter wears his Skeet vest over a plastic windcheater.

Do not skimp on the gloves you buy for shooting. They should fit like a second skin and be as thin as possible.

because of their flat soles, they allow my weight to come back very slightly. Moreover, they are quite unsuited to cold or wet conditions. You should also own a good-quality pair of wellington boots, and some high but not excessively thick socks.

Accessories

Every Sporting shooter needs some sort of bag in which to carry his cartridges and other kit. Some prefer to have a cartridge bag and a separate hold-all. I noted in the safety chapter that it

Every shooter will need a cartridge bag of some sort. The one on the right was made to my own specification and includes a pouch for sunglasses.

The new Remington peerless over and under could make a useful sporter.

is sensible to carry spare ear-plugs or muffs. A small towel will also come in handy on wet days or when your hands are sweating. Gloves are another consideration; in really cold weather they can be very useful. If you buy gloves, buy the best and thinnest you can. Some shots use gloves all the time; my own preference is for bare hands for a better feel of the gun. I usually buy thin gloves a size too small because, invariably, they stretch.

Anything else? Carry a first-aid kit and a notebook in your car. You will also find it useful to have a cleaning rod and a small tool kit for your gun. If you have a gun with an adjustable trigger locked by a screw, write to the manufacturer and ask them to send you a couple of spare screws – they have a nasty habit of falling out when you least expect it. If you have a multichoke gun, you will find an improved choke changer (as made by various companies) a big improvement on the tatty and sharp bits of metal that most manufacturers supply. Older shooters may find a portable stool, possibly one incorporating a kit bag or box, very useful when they are forced to wait for long periods at major shoots.

4 Fundamentals

THE UNIVERSALS OF GOOD SHOOTING

There are certain principles that are common to all good shotgun marksmanship, no matter which specific technique or style is employed. First is *discipline*. In all forms of shooting, poor performance is often a result of sloppiness, of not doing what you know you should have been doing. *Motivation* is also important: wanting to do well. But good discipline and motivation are rather general; we can focus in on three specifics – the Universals – for all good shotgun shooting: *visual contact, balance and rhythm*. I find it useful to picture them as a triangle, with visual contact at the top, the focus of all one's effort.

Considered together, the Universals create a concept of *the whole shooter*, which is the basis of my system of shotgun instruction and fault

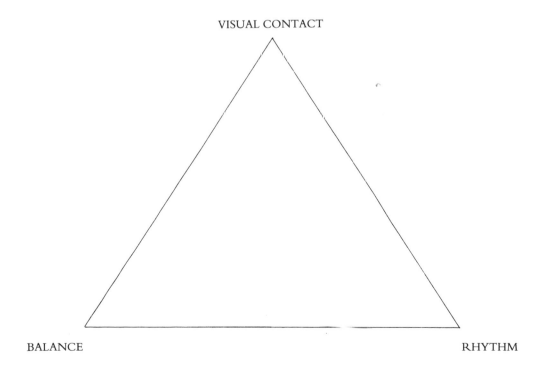

VISUAL CONTACT

BALANCE

RHYTHM

The Universals – principles of good shooting.

The Universals Explained

Visual contact

Visual contact is an index of concentration. It involves gluing your eyes on to the target from the point of first visual pick-up and maintaining focus on the target until it is just a puff of smoke or a collection of fragments. This is much easier said than done. Watching the target properly is a skill which must be learned. Without training, most people's focus will wander between the gun and the target.

Balance

Balance means maintaining a stance which is comfortable, stable and which promotes a smooth swing. You must find a stance which is comfortable and effective for you. Depending on the shooting method you employ, this may change, however, from one type of shot to another. My own preference for most shots is the Stanbury style of stance, where the weight stays on the ball of the front foot (the left foot for right-handed, right-master-eyed shots) throughout the process of shooting. This will not work for everyone and you must experiment to find out what works best for you.

Rhythm

Rhythm is hard to put into words precisely; sometimes people call it timing. Essentially rhythm is the business of shooting as if to a beat. For example, the rhythm of shooting high-driven birds is well expressed by the old gamekeeper's phrase, *You ... Are ... Dead*. The shooter says 'You' on first visual contact, 'Are' as the gun comes up, and 'Dead' as the trigger is pulled. Most Sporting birds, live and artificial, are shot to three beats, but the

A balanced starting position. Note the position of the feet, the weight distribution and the line of sight running just above the muzzles.

tempo changes according to the shot. On a close quartering target, the tempo will be quite fast; on a long crosser, the tempo will be fairly slow.

For more on the Universals, *see* pages 86–9.

correction. The perfect shot – which we all should aspire to be – would have complete mastery of all three Universals in any circumstance. Conversely, poor performance on any of the Universals – though we may get away with it occasionally – means we are not shooting as well as we might. Improvement in our performance on the Universals will be dependent upon: *awareness* of their importance and the *consistent* application of sound technique. Think about it now: how does your shooting measure up when judged against the Universals? Do you maintain good visual contact? Is your stance stable throughout the swing? Do you think your timing might be improved?

Safety apart, sustained visual contact with the target is the single most important thing in shotgun marksmanship.

THE MASTER EYE

Before we can progress to any exercises for improving shooting it is important to establish which is your master eye. Some people struggle on for years not hitting very much, utterly unaware that they have a master eye problem which is making them shoot to one side of all their targets.

Even if you think you know which is your master eye, test for it again now

Take the cardboard tube from a roll of kitchen or lavatory paper (or make a circle by bringing together the thumb and index finger of one hand). Pick out a small but distinct spot on the wall or horizon and, keeping both eyes open and holding the tube about a foot from your face look at the spot through the tube. Now, shut your right eye (if you are right-handed); has the spot moved from the centre of the tube? If so, you are probably right master-eyed. If you can still see the object through the tube, you are probably left master-eyed.

What does all this mean? If you are right-handed and right master-eyed, you have no problems; similarly if you are left-handed and left master-eyed. The difficulty is when one's 'handedness' and master eye are opposite. A right-hander with a left master eye has a number of options: the best, I believe, is to learn to shoot off the other shoulder, something which may seem a little awkward initially but, usually, is quickly adjusted to. The great advantage to learning to shoot off the other shoulder if you have handedness opposite to your master eye, is that it allows you to keep both eyes open and thus gain all the important advantages of binocular vision. Shotgun shooting is more natural and more efficient using both eyes.

For those who cannot adapt to shooting off the wrong shoulder, there are other options.

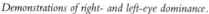
Demonstrations of right- and left-eye dominance.

These include dimming or closing the outboard eye as the gun is mounted (a procedure which allows the shooter to take some advantage of binocular vision. Alternatively, an eye patch can be worn (not recommended unless you enjoy looking like Long John Silver), or a vision barrier can be fixed to the appropriate lens of a pair of prescription or protective spectacles. Yet another remedy (I would not bother with this one either) is to attach a vision-blocking device to the barrels themselves: 'obturator' handguards used to be made for side-by-sides and had a small disc positioned to obstruct the vision of the left eye; in the United States, the 'Blinder' is currently available, which attaches to either side of an over-and-under gun just behind the muzzles.

The old, expensive, remedy for master eye problems was to acquire a cross-over stock gun. Such a gun has a stock with a very obvious S-bend, which allows the shooter to mount the gun on one shoulder whilst aligning the barrels with a master eye on the opposite side. I do not like these guns much, shooting is hard enough work as it is without being forced to use such an ungainly contraption. Moreover, as far as over-and-unders are concerned, it is all a bit academic anyway; they are very rarely made with cross-over stocks. The only over-and-under cross-over gun I am familiar with handled poorly and kicked like a mule.

There is more to the question of eye dominance than the simple discovery that someone is right- or left-eye dominant. A few people will have so-called 'central vision,' where neither eye is truly dominant. Others will have one eye only slightly more dominant than the other. These subtle differences in vision – which will normally require the assistance of an experienced instructor/gunfitter to diagnose – will have the effect of pulling the muzzles to one side of the target or the other if the shooter is in the habit of keeping both eyes open. Although I believe that the best route for anyone suffering from 'cross dominance' is to learn to shoot off the opposite shoulder, this remedy will not, of course, work for those suffering from central vision and other conditions which involve less than absolute dominance in one eye.

Here (and for anyone who cannot adjust to opposite shoulder shooting) a physical block to the vision of one eye is essential: either the simple procedure of closing or dimming the appropriate eye as the gun is mounted, or one of the mechanical vision blocks described above. If you opt for modifying a pair of spectacles – and this is the best course if you cannot adapt to shooting off the opposite shoulder or squinting an eye – do not make the visual block too large. The block only needs to be large enough to obstruct the pupil reliably – no more than ½in (1cm). Some shooters blank out the whole of one lens, quite unnecessarily; all that is required is a small spot which will block the vision of the offending eye when the head is in its shooting position on the stock. To place the dot accurately on the spectacles, enlist the help of a friend equipped with some self-adhesive spots (circular target patches or pricing labels are ideal).

Having proved the gun empty, mount it as normal at an imaginary target on the horizon. Ask the friend (who should be standing on the same side as the lens requiring attention) to position the spot so that its centre matches the centre of your pupil.

Once completed, the modified spectacles will seem almost normal when worn, and the spot will be barely noticeable. The glasses will allow you to see the target initially with two eyes, thus getting all the distance judging and tracking benefits of binocular vision, but they will block out the confusing image of the second eye as the gun comes into the face and shoulder.

I will conclude by noting that many right-handed women do not have right master eyes. Moreover, the eye dominance of men often

changes in middle age. It can also be affected by long-distance driving or prolonged work at a computer terminal. If you have any concern on the question of eye dominance find someone who really knows his stuff and get him to check you out.

I also routinely advise my students to have their vision tested by an optician, and to follow this up with a test every two or three years (annually if they are over sixty). The right pair of corrective lenses can make an enormous difference to the shooting performance of those with less than perfect vision. It is not just a question of testing to see if your eyes can see detail at distance. Someone who can see detail

A spot placed on the lens of prescription or protective glasses can overcome an eye dominance problem, but take care not to make the spot larger than it needs to be.

at a distance, who has so-called 20:20 vision, may have problems with binocular balance, with tracking moving objects, and with the speed of focusing to mention but a few points. Do not put off having an eye test even if you think you have perfect vision. The importance of good natural or corrected vision in shooting cannot be overemphasized.

SHOOTING TECHNIQUE

Having considered certain basic principles applicable to all shotgun marksmanship, and discovered which is our master eye, we may now consider, briefly and without prejudice, some of the basic techniques of shooting.

First, we might note that to hit a moving target it is necessary to shoot in front of it. Few could argue with that statement, but there has been endless debate on how to achieve the right lead. Some authorities will tell you to apply forward allowance consciously, others will tell you to watch the bird and forget everything else – the subconscious mind or the momentum of the gun will do all the work for you. Further, there are those who advocate that the barrels of the gun should 'swing through' the target from behind (this is sometimes called the smoke-trail method); there are others who suggest that the barrels should 'move with the bird' and then accelerate in front of it; there are some who say you should always 'maintain lead', i.e. keep the barrels ahead of the target throughout the process of shooting. A few even advocate trying to 'intercept' the target by shooting at a specific spot in front of it.

Argument about technique does not end with the great lead debate. Various opinions have also been expressed as to how one should stand when shooting, and upon the subject of how the gun should be brought to the shoulder.

Stance

One school of thought suggests that for most shots, you should take up a position nearly square to the target with the weight evenly distributed; another will tell you to stand nearly square to the target and shift your weight according to the shot. The most common recommendation is that one should stand oblique to the target with the bulk of the weight on the front foot for all, or nearly all, shots. Most traditionally trained shotgun instructors in Britain teach that the feet should not be too wide apart. The advice that the feet should be kept 'shoulder width' apart is often heard in clay shooting circles. This is hard to define precisely, although the general principle is apparent: someone of narrow build should stand with his feet closer together than someone of wide build.

Mounting and Holding the Gun

The great majority of shooting instructors advocate a gun-down position for Sporting birds, that is the gun butt should not be in the shoulder when the target is called for. Disagreements arise over exactly where the butt and barrels should be placed.

Some advocate a fairly low starting position for the butt of the gun for all Sporting shooting, similar to the position many game shooters adopt. Others, the majority, suggest that the top of the butt should be just under or about level with the armpit. Instructors influenced by Robert Churchill's methods may suggest that the butt should nestle under the armpit and be gently squeezed between bicep and rib. This position, they say, will force the shooter to push the gun out and bring it into the right place in the shoulder, which most would agree is the 'shoulder pocket' – the natural hollow between the collar bone and the shoulder joint.

On the subject of barrel position, most would say that, as far as clay shooting is concerned, the barrels should start pointed at, or in front of, the point of first visual contact with the target. However, some instructors will tell you to bring your muzzles up to the line of the bird as you prepare to shoot, so that you may instantly establish a relation with the target when it appears. Others will tell you to leave the muzzles well down, as they claim that a high muzzle position will obscure the bird and force you to chop under its line of flight.

CONCLUSIONS

For both the novice and the experienced shot, all this apparent contradiction is, to say the least, rather confusing. One book says one thing, another something completely different. Who is right? I think most successful competitors at Sporting Clays would agree that to shoot at the highest level requires mastery of more than a single technique (at least as far as forward allowance is concerned). I suspect most of them would also agree that no one is going to be able to apply a variety of techniques unless he has learnt one of them really well. For the moment,

we are only going to consider a single, well-proven and simple way to shoot: the Positive Shooting method. It draws from many sources and has been developed after many years' study and application of the classic styles, particularly those taught by Percy Stanbury and Robert Churchill; I have also been much impressed by the simplicity and clarity of the CPSA method. I do not claim that the Positive Shooting method is the only way to shoot, but I believe it is a good way for many people, and I suggest that you try it and see if it works for you. Even if you do not get on with it in its entirety, you may find some of its features useful.

Essentially, the Positive Shooting method is a mating of Stanbury's footwork to Churchill's lead system, but in a package which promotes consistent shooting under the pressure of competition. Something very like the Positive Shooting method is used by 80 per cent of successful clay shooters. It is not a perfect way to shoot every target – there is no such thing – but it is simple and works for most people on most targets. The Positive Shooting method will provide most shooters with a solid foundation from which to develop a personal style.

5 The Positive Shooting Method

The Positive Shooting method stresses the importance of preparation. It boils down to this: Assess the line of the target before shooting. Establish: (a) where you first see the target as a blur or streak as it exits the trap; (b) where you first see it clearly as a solid object; and (c) where, approximately, you want to kill it. Set up your stance according to the chosen 'killing point' (which will normally be the spot where the shooter may first kill the target comfortably). Mount the gun (rules permitting) on to it, visualize the target breaking, and wind the muzzles back along the line of flight, stopping at the point of first clear visual contact. Lower the butt from the shoulder, keeping the tip of the muzzles just under the line of flight. Now direct your eyes a little further back along the line of flight to the area where the target is first seen as a blur or streak. Call for the target and, as soon as you see it, start the gun and upper body moving. Lock your eyes on to the leading edge of the target. Pull the trigger when you sense the lead is correct, keeping your eyes locked on to the leading edge of the target all the time.

A key concept of the Positive Shooting method is that once the technique has been learnt, *deliberate* forward allowance is not required on most targets. The correct lead will be applied subconsciously, or semiconsciously as long as there has been proper preparation and as long as visual contact and good rhythm are sustained while shooting.

THE BASIC MOUNT

No matter what the technique, a good gun mount is the foundation stone of good shoot-

ing; even the most experienced shots need to practise it. Let us imagine that we are going to shoot at a static target immediately to our front and just above the horizon. (The following instructions are intended for a right-handed shooter; left-handers should follow the same procedure, but substitute 'left' for 'right'.) The front foot will be at approximately one o'clock to the target, the rear foot at approximately three o'clock (eleven o'clock and nine o'clock for left-handers). The gap between the heels will be between six and eight inches. The rear heel will be slightly raised. Your weight should be forward, the bulk of it on the ball of the front foot. You should not lean forward from the waist like some Trap shooters do (it will make it hard to swing the gun.) Rather, imagine a line going down through your leading shoulder, via the hip to the ball of the leading foot. Your weight is going through that line.

The heel of the butt will usually be held beneath the armpit with the top edge of the comb slightly above the forearm. The muzzles should be held up, but not too high, with the tip of the barrels just under an imaginary line from the eye to the target. The muzzles must *not* be placed above the line of the bird at any time (if they are, there will be a tendency to chop down as the gun is mounted).

The right hand will maintain a comfortable but firm grip on the gun with the web between thumb and index finger located just to the top right side of the grip, and not precisely on the top of the grip. Correct positioning of the hand ensures that the elbow falls into a comfortable, unstrained position and that the index finger can be extended without twisting. The area on

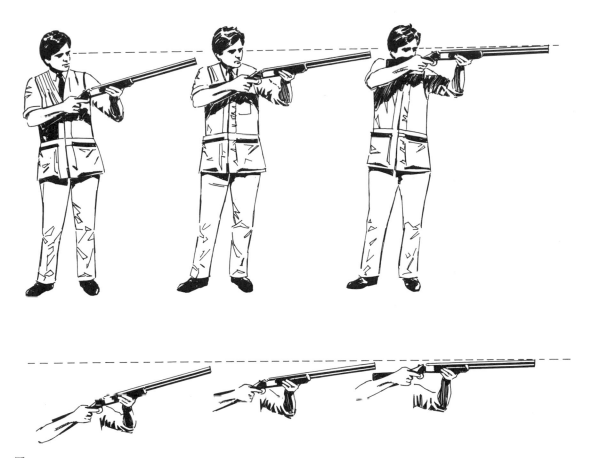

The mount.

the index finger between the pad and the first joint will make contact with the trigger.

The left hand will be in a comfortable mid-way position on the fore-end and not gripping too hard (although the gentle but firm control exerted by the left hand and arm is crucial). The fore-end is held with the fingers and not rested in the palm. The left-hand index finger will be pointing towards the target, and will be placed along the bottom left-hand edge of the fore-end. Both elbows will be naturally positioned pointing at about 45 degrees to the ground.

The gun stock should be raised to the face and shoulder with a co-ordinated movement of both hands. The head, which is held almost erect but with the chin very slightly down, remains still throughout the movement. As the stock comes to the face, the comb locates under the arch of the cheekbone. The face is in positive contact with the wood but is not squashed down.

A good mount involves fluid and rhythmical body movements. It is an unhurried action. During the mount, the gun will pivot about the axis of the muzzles, it will also be pushed towards the target. Both hands move in concert, but the arc of movement of the rear hand is slightly greater than that of the front. As the gun rises, the shoulder rises naturally, too, and is pushed forward slightly to meet the sole of the gun butt. I would emphasize that this is not an exaggerated movement.

The mount: side view.

The mount: front view.

70

THE MOUNT AND SWING

The basic mount just described involves no lateral movement. It is a useful training exercise, but in the field it would only be applicable to those birds that are going away or approaching the shooter in a perfectly straight line. Most targets will require a lateral 'swinging' motion as well.

The process is exactly the same as that for the basic mount, except that after setting up the stance to the approximate killing point (which, as noted, is usually the first place where the bird may comfortably be shot), the shooter must rotate the upper body and gun back towards the point where the target is first seen as a solid object.

As far as lead is concerned, the theoretical ideal, with this system, is to make the muzzles travel with the bird as the swing begins, moving them smoothly in front of the mount and swing progress. In practice, the shooter may not always achieve this. Sometimes the barrels will move with the target from the start, as they should; sometimes they may end up maintaining a lead. Sometimes, when the shooter has reacted poorly to the bird, they may come through from behind. As long as you have filed the thought away that the barrels *ought* to begin with the bird, do not worry – what really counts is maintaining visual contact with the target, not arguments about what system you shoot.

PUTTING IT INTO PRACTICE

I have never believed in just going out and 'shooting a few' with an instructor whose only function is to give the odd useful tip. Too often, in such circumstances, the shooter finds his shooting is improved during the coaching session but reverts to mediocrity afterwards. I suspect there are two reasons for this. One is that the shooter does not know why he is going

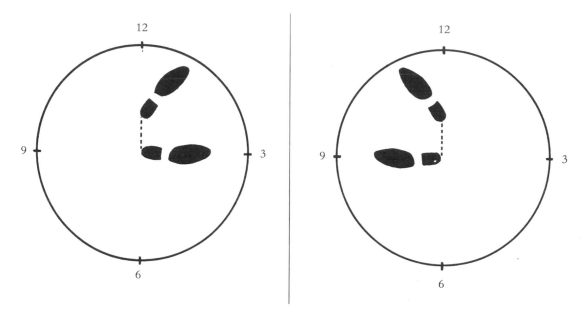

Ideal foot positions.

A comfortable hand position is very important. Note the location on the grip of the thumb relative to the other fingers.

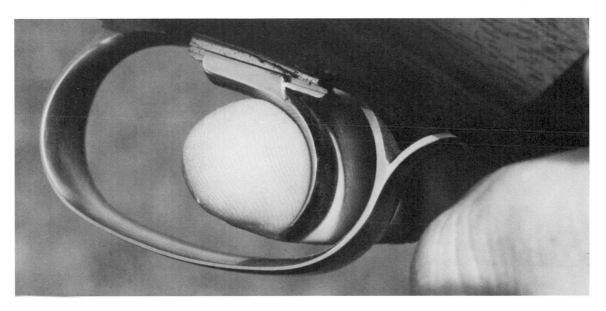

The correct position for the trigger: between the pad and the first joint of the index finger.

If you place your thumb behind the top lever, it can sustain a painful injury from the recoil.

wrong because he has never been formally taught precisely what to do; and the other, and related, reason is that the shooter is not performing on the basis of a disciplined routine. When you are taught in an off-the-cuff sort of way, you tend to perform in a similar fashion. I believe that most shooters will benefit from a much more systematic approach to their shotgun marksmanship. A well-learned (and taught) technique gives them something to fall back on when things go wrong; the purely instinctual shot never has the same advantage. Moreover, why waste years half-learning how to shoot?

This is how to kill a simple crossing target using the Positive Shooting technique. As with all shots and all techniques, there are two stages to be considered: *preparation* and *performance*.

Elbow position. The correct position for the elbows is to have both at approximately 45 degrees to the ground. Some Trap shooters favour a higher elbow position for the rear arm, but this tends to interfere with the swing when shooting Sporting targets from a gun-down position.

Preparation

1. Watch a few birds to see how they are flying. Ask yourself, 'Is the line of speed of the bird deceptive?' (It will be useful to watch others shooting to determine this.)

2. Note where you first see the bird as a blur, and the point where you first see it distinctly as a clay target.

3. Consider a 'killing point' – the first point where the bird may comfortably be shot. Do not make a final decision until you have moved into your actual shooting position.

Performance

1. Choose your killing point and set up your stance to it: front foot at one o'clock, rear foot at three o'clock (eleven o'clock and nine o'clock for left-handers). Mount the gun (rules permitting) on your intended killing point.

2. Visualize the target being killed.

3. Keeping the gun in the shoulder (again, rules permitting) rotate back along the line of the flight to the point where the target is first seen distinctly. (If the rules stipulate a gun-down start, rotate back in the address position

Always take advantage of the opportunity to watch the birds before you shoot.

but still being careful to keep the muzzles just under the line of the bird.)

4. Drop the butt from the shoulder, keeping the muzzles just under the line of flight.

5. Turning your head slightly, direct your eyes to the area where the target is first seen as a blur or streak and call for your target.

6. As soon as you see the target, start the upper body and gun moving.

7. The focus is centred on the leading edge of the clay, and the muzzles, directed by the co-ordinated action of both hands, move ahead naturally as the gun swings.

8. Fire the gun as the butt comes firmly into the face and shoulder, and as the correct lead picture is seen subconsciously or semi-consciously (the shoulder will have been brought slightly forward, and the muscles of the shoulder, neck and hands will have tensed at the moment of firing).

9. Follow through, maintaining visual contact with the broken target.

Take a piece of card and write or type the stages of preparation and performance on it now. It will not be practical to remember all of them immediately. However, there are some key points (which might be written down on the reverse of the card, together with the triangle of Universals), which should be committed to memory and consciously performed every time you shoot. I call them the 'The Four As':

(a) If possible, watch the target before shooting it.

(b) Establish where you see the target as a blur, where you first see it as a solid object, and approximately where you want to kill it.

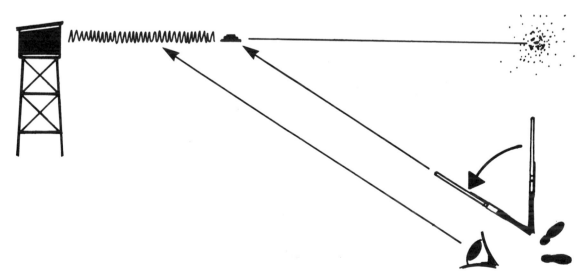

(c) Set your stance towards the killing point; rules permitting, mount the gun on to it and wind back along the line of flight to the point where you first see the target as a solid object. Keeping the muzzles just under the line, lower the butt from the shoulder and direct your eyes to where you first see the target as a blur.

The Four As

Always assess your target, noting its line and where you first see it as a blur, and where you first see it clearly.

Always select a killing point and set your stance according to it.

Always visualize what you want to achieve – a kill – before you shoot.

Always maintain visual contact throughout the act of shooting.

Of all the above, the last is the most important.

Developing a shooting routine based on a sound technique will immediately increase your percentage of kills, and it will help you to identify mistakes by establishing a datum against which you can compare actual performance. Once a routine like this becomes truly habitual, the shooter will progress to a new level of competence.

We have noted that if you follow a systematic approach to shooting, which puts special emphasis on preparation, you will not have to worry too much about lead on the great majority of targets. As long as you have the determination to keep your eyes glued to the target, lead calculation will become regulated almost automatically after adequate training. I say after adequate training, because a more conscious approach to lead will always be required in the initial stages of learning.

We have also noted that there are certain exceptions to the unconscious approach. These

are worth considering briefly now. High-driven birds, some long crossing targets, and some visually deceptive targets may well require a slightly more deliberate technique. However, it will rarely amount to more than saying to oneself in the preparation phase, 'This one needs a little extra' or 'I must make an effort to shoot under this one'. No precise measuring off of the target will be required. Measuring off rarely leads to consistent shooting – and is not advocated here – because the angle, speed and distance of the targets vary too much for the technique to be consistently applied.

Common Errors

As you begin to put the Positive Shooting method into practice, you may find your errors have a distinct pattern. You may make the effort to align yourself to the killing point, or place your muzzles in the correct starting position for the first few shots, only to find that your concentration wanes and your foot and muzzle positions with it. Visualize yourself now setting up your body for a crossing shot to your front.

The left foot is at one o'clock to the anticipated killing point, the right foot at three o'clock (opposite stance for left-handers). Mount the gun onto the killing point. Visualize the clay being smoked. Wind back along the line of flight to the point of first clear visual contact; drop the butt. *Pull!* Your eyes grab the target, the muzzles lock onto it like the guidance system of a computer-controlled missile, you concentrate on the leading edge. As the gun butt rises to the face, the barrels are moving in front of the target . . . the trigger is pulled . . . the target is broken . . . the gun barrels continue to move.

6 Other Shooting Techniques

Having considered the Positive Shooting technique, we may now consider some of the other well-known ways to shoot. They will be useful both for interest and for experiment as you develop your own style; I would never suggest that only one technique will suit everyone on all targets.

THE STANBURY METHOD

The Positive Shooting technique owes much to the Stanbury Method, which is the technique devised by the legendary English shot Percy Stanbury (for many years Chief Instructor at the West London Shooting Grounds), and set down by him and Gordon Carlisle in their famous books *Shotgun Marksmanship* and *Clay Pigeon Marksmanship*. The Positive Shooting method shares the same foot position – one o'clock and three o'clock to the target; and the same weight distribution – the bulk of the weight to be kept on the front foot (and specifically the ball of the front foot) regardless of the shot. However, Positive Shooting places more emphasis on aligning oneself to the killing point, and on pre-shot preparation.

There are other differences. Stanbury suggests a more deliberate approach to lead than I would. He talks about 'seeing' and learning various 'lead pictures'. I resort to this system on occasion but, generally speaking, have found it to be less consistent than the unconscious approach (except on certain very long or very deceptive targets as already noted).

Taking a high bird the Stanbury way. Notice the weight is on the front foot.

THE CHURCHILL METHOD

Robert Churchill was a famous London gunmaker who was celebrated for his books on shooting style, his 25in barrelled 'XXV' gun, and his colourful performances in the witness

78

box as a firearms expert for Scotland Yard. Churchill stated that the 'old–fashioned' way of deliberately swinging through a bird and seeing lead was a waste of time. The essence of his method is that the shooter should swing on to the bird, trust his eye to make the necessary forward allowance subconsciously and, to quote his biographer Macdonald Hastings, 'leave the gun to do the rest'. Like his 25in guns, his theories of marksmanship caused a great deal of controversy.

Before going further, let me make it clear that Churchill never taught that one should shoot at the bird; rather he stated that with a good mounting technique, and by pointing the left hand at the bird, it would *seem* as if one were shooting at the bird. This point is explained in his book *How to Shoot* (*see* Further Reading) from which this extract is taken:

The whole secret is to regularize your movements and mount the gun properly to the shoulder so that the hand and eye co-ordinate. Your barrel must always be aligned precisely where your eye is looking. The eye learns its job quickly enough. Apparently you are shooting straight at the bird, but unconsciously you will be making the necessary forward allowance.

Churchill has been much misunderstood. I largely agree with his comments on lead but, as with his advocacy of the XXV gun, I think he overstates his case. His suggestion that lead should never be applied consciously goes a little too far. One may shoot, with good preparation, without conscious lead 90 per cent, perhaps even 95 per cent of the time, but not always. Some of the targets on a modern Sporting layout (and some live birds) require a more conscious approach.

Churchill also suggested footwork which was very different to the classic Lancaster/ Stanbury approach. Here, I am less of a supporter. Churchill would have the shooter stand almost square to the target, transferring the

The Churchill technique for taking a high bird to the right. Notice the weight transference to the right (rear) foot.

weight to the left foot for a shot going to the left, to the right for a shot going to the right. The system works quite well for people of heavy, rather squat build like Churchill himself, but is not, I believe, to be generally recommended. Nevertheless, Churchill's book, *Game Shooting*, in which he discusses his technique in detail, is a classic which should be on every serious shooter's bookshelf. (*See* Further Reading.)

THE HOLLAND & HOLLAND METHOD

Churchill's master coach was a man called

Ken Davies of Holland & Holland demonstrates the Churchill mount, with the cone of the gunstock positioned underneath the armpit. This starting position forces the shooter to push the gun out when mounting it to the shoulder.

Norman Clarke who went to work for Holland & Holland and taught Holland's great modern coach, Ken Davies. Ken, who like many first-rate coaches, has a flexible approach, now teaches a method which combines Churchill's footwork with an undogmatic approach to lead. An interesting feature of both the pure Churchill method and the Holland/Clarke/Davies hybrid is that the mount is commenced with the butt positioned under the armpit, which forces the shooter to bring the gun forward and back to seat into the shoulder pocket. Although this looks rather odd, I have found that it helps some people with chronic gun-mounting problems, although I prefer not to exaggerate the starting position as much as Churchill did. The gun may be held with the heel of the stock just under the front edge of the armpit, rather than pulled further back as Churchill did.

THE CPSA METHOD

The Clay Pigeon Shooting Association (CPSA) has developed its own excellent and very simple method for teaching people to shoot. The CPSA method might be summed up in the words: *pick it up; pull ahead; shoot.* The shooter mounts onto the bird, tracks it gun in shoulder, then consciously moves ahead and fires. The CPSA method does not advocate holding or 'measuring off' a specific lead picture, the trigger is instinctively pulled at the right moment as the gun accelerates in front of the target.

The advantage to the CPSA technique is that one may, as one tracks, quite accurately assess the speed of a bird. The disadvantage is that it is a relatively slow process which involves extended tracking with a mounted gun. I do not think this encourages a good rhythm.

Moreover, the method is clearly limited in its applications, and I cannot imagine anyone's using it successfully at Olympic Skeet or Olympic Trap. Nevertheless, it is an excellent system for teaching beginners how to deal with crossing targets. It is especially useful when instructional time is limited.

MOVE, MOUNT, SHOOT – JOHN BIDWELL

Former World Sporting Champion, John Bidwell, has developed his own method of shooting which he calls Move, Mount, Shoot. It is a maintained lead method (that is, a technique where the gun barrels stay ahead of the target throughout the shooting process), but of a new sort. The beauty of John's technique is that, like the CPSA method, it is very simple. The shooter starts with the gun butt fairly low down and also with the muzzles well below the line of the target. The correct starting position for the muzzles in the horizontal plane is about halfway between the trap and the intended killing point.

As with other techniques, as soon as visual contact is made with the target the gun starts to move (this is particularly crucial with Move, Mount, Shoot). As with Churchill, no conscious lead calculation is made, although one should be aware that the muzzles of the gun must stay ahead of the target throughout the shooting process. I like the technique and I think it deserves more attention, although I would not recommend it for rabbits or springing teal. I find that on some targets – especially long crossers – many shots naturally adopt a form of maintained lead, although not necessarily with a low gun start position. Another,

John Bidwell instructing.

sometimes very useful, advantage to maintained lead techniques is that they allow the target to be broken more quickly than with other methods. One of the most common errors when people start learning John's technique is to fail to start the gun moving as soon as the bird is seen.

AMERICAN MAINTAINED LEAD

Whilst discussing maintained lead, we might also note the very deliberate version of this style used by many American Skeet shooters. As they pass from station to station they will actually say, 'Well, this bird needs eighteen inches, that one two feet.' Their form of maintained lead is based on specific calculations and a fully mounted gun; it is quite different from John Bidwell's. It will only work when birds are presented at known distances and angles. The best-known modern exponent of this method is Ed Scherer, his latest book, *Scherer on Skeet, II* is well worth reading.

SPOT SHOOTING

Another technique used by American Skeet shooters, but also by some hopeful hunters and clay shots, is 'spot shooting', sometimes called interception. Let us imagine a bird going from left to right. The shooter will select a spot along its line and decide to pull the trigger just before the bird gets there. Because he is not swinging with the bird, his chances of success are unpredictable. But before I rubbish the idea of spot shooting completely, I will note that there are (rare) occasions when one has few options: for example, when in a Sporting competition there is a rabbit which must be shot between two posts, with the view of the rabbit obstructed until it reaches the first post. In this sort of circumstance, one has little choice but to try some sort of spot shooting.

TRAP SHOOTING

A few brief words on Trap Shooting technique are in order here because, occasionally, it will make sense to apply a Trap-like technique to a Trap-like bird encountered at Sporting. There are a variety of techniques for Trap Shooting, but they all have in common a pre-mounted gun. Although there are disadvantages to a pre-mounted gun on most Sporting targets (since it may impede visual contact and timing), there are certain English Sporting targets where a pre-mounted, or very nearly mounted, gun can be useful – for example some long-range quartering targets similar in angle to Trap birds. Experience will teach you which targets will benefit from this approach.

When shooting pre-mounted, or nearly pre-mounted, the basics still apply. Visual Contact, Balance, Rhythm (although the rhythm is quite different – Trap birds are usually shot to two beats). A wide variety of stances is used for Trap Shooting, but the feet are typically positioned fairly close together to promote a more fluid swing. Most Trap shooters advocate aligning themselves to favour the extreme left- and right-handed targets on stands 1 and 5. The illustration shows the normal pick-up points at Down the Line (DTL).

Never dwell on a target when shooting pre-mounted; fire as soon as your eyes are locked on to the target. Though a few might argue the point, no conscious lead should be needed.

Even though the shooter mounts before calling for the target, consistency of mount is paramount to success (which is why some Trap guns have an extra centre bead on the gun to ensure precise alignment). Apart from inconsistent gun mounting, common errors in Trap Shooting include: poor reaction to the target, failing to maintain or adequately establish visual contact, squashing the cheek too far down on the stock, allowing the neck to creep forward on the stock, being too deliberate in one's shooting technique and, not least, head raising – 'looking over the gun' – as it is fired.

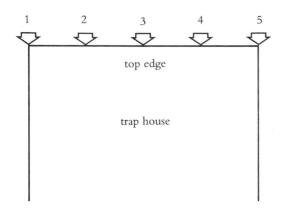

This diagram shows where the shooter should start pointing his gun barrels when Trap shooting. The numbers on the top edge of the trap house correspond to the shooting position being stood upon. Some shooters start pointing at 3 from all positions, some favour a higher holding position and there are other variations too. Nevertheless, I find that these hold points work well for most people.

One other point worth making is that many Trap shooters adopt a high position for the right elbow. This position expands the so-called 'shoulder pocket' but is, in my opinion, unsuited to any Sporting application because it tends to impede the swing on crossing targets.

SELF-TAUGHT SPORTING TECHNIQUE

Before finishing this section I might note one more 'technique' that some Sporting Clay shooters adopt. It is most clearly identified by a stance which involves standing almost, or absolutely, square to the target with the feet wide apart, often with a pre-mounted or nearly pre-mounted gun. It might be combined with any lead system. I think it looks awful (as bad as the 'lavatory crouch' in Olympic Skeet shooting),

Shooting over the top of the bird is a very common Trap shooting error (another is poor pick-up). For this reason, I tell novices to shoot just beneath the target and without hesitation. Speed of swing takes care of lead for 80 per cent of people.

These three highly experienced shooters all show slight variations of personal style, but note their relaxed concentration and the position of their muzzles, which is, in all cases, just below their line of sight.

but some very successful, self-taught, shooters adopt this wide, square stance. I have to admit to experimenting with this sort of stance recently, and to discovering that it can provide a very stable platform for some shots (for example, long crossers in very windy conditions). I would not use such a stance for all my shooting, but, inelegant or not, it can evidently be effective in some circumstances. Any shot who wants to improve should risk experimenting with unfamiliar techniques.

CONCLUSIONS

As already noted, the time to consider different techniques comes after the shooter has mastered one of them. I advocate the Positive Shooting method as a starting point, but I believe that if you want to shoot well you must, eventually, be able to apply a variety of techniques. For advanced shooters, it is a particularly useful training exercise to apply different systems of forward allowance to the same bird. Try shooting a simple crosser with the Swing-Through system, with specific maintained leads, with John Bidwell's technique, with the CPSA method and by interception as well as with the Positive Shooting method. This sort of exercise helps the shooter to develop control, and to find the style that suits him best on specific targets. As I have implied throughout this book, nothing concerning shooting technique is written in tablets of stone. If you want to improve your shooting, you must experiment.

7 Training Aids and Fault Diagnosis

Perhaps the best training aid of all is a coach whom you trust. Finding such a person may not be easy, and it may be an expensive undertaking if he works on a professional rather than an amateur basis. It goes without saying that it is important to find someone who is both skilled and with whom you can develop a good rapport. Usually, money spent on coaching or instruction is well spent. Group tuition or shooting courses, as offered by the BASC, CPSA and SRA, are a good compromise.

Another excellent training aid is to shoot with a friend, preferably one who is a better shot than you are. As we have already noted, one of the quickest ways to improve is to seek out people who shoot really well, and there is no better place to find them than at a good Sporting club.

Every shooter will benefit from regular practice with a friend whose judgement he trusts. Here, the shooter in front appears to have raised his head slightly, which may cause a miss above the clay.

Every shooter should seek out a professional instructor at some stage in his shooting career. Here are two masters of the craft, Alan Rose and Richard Ford, demonstrating the different approaches required for different students.

A shooting partner is useful because he can encourage you to keep up a training schedule, and can also act as a coach. Even though it makes sense to seek out professional help if you have a persistent problem, there is a great deal that two well-informed friends can do to help one another, particularly if they remember the principles set out in the three Universals of good shooting: *visual contact, balance* and *rhythm*. With coaching in mind, let us consider each of them again:

Visual contact Even the best shots sometimes lose or fail to achieve adequate visual contact with the target. There are many ways to improve visual discipline. Having someone behind telling you to 'watch the target' can be effective, especially in the early stages of learning. Reminding yourself to keep looking at the target, and especially the leading edge – which might be the front, top or bottom of the bird – rather than just a vague shape, is also important.

87

All of us must, eventually, become 'self-reinforcing' if we wish to succeed. A good shooting routine, which includes a precise strategy for directing the eyes to a pick-up-zone, is vital because it sets us up to lock onto the target quickly and efficiently.

Balance Balance involves maintaining a stance which is comfortable, stable and which promotes a smooth swing. Everyone must find a stance which is comfortable and effective for him. Good balance will allow the shooter to move smoothly with the target and to control recoil. Poor balance is instantly recognizable because the shooter will be inconsistent, frequently swinging off the line of the target and failing to control recoil. Balance will be easier to achieve in a position which is comfortable and which suits the physique of the shooter. Good balance is rarely achieved in Sporting shooting with exaggerated or ungainly body positions.

Balance can be improved by the adoption of a good basic technique, and further enhanced by practice on awkward targets and on awkward ground. Balance can also be improved by physical fitness. In shooting, strong arms and shoulders are obviously important, but so are strong legs. Exercises such as swimming, running, and cycling will improve balance and general fitness, as will games like tennis and badminton, which have the added advantage of improving hand–eye co-ordination. Physical fitness will be considered in more detail in Chapter 9 (*see* pages 124–7).

Rhythm This is the hardest of the Universals to put into words precisely. Essentially, good rhythm concerns the business of shooting smoothly, as if to a beat. Good rhythm is unhurried and promotes both an elegant style and consistency.

Cultivating a good rhythm is one of the hardest and most important skills of shooting, and one that is little considered in modern writing on instructional technique – no doubt because it is so difficult to describe. The first stage of developing a good rhythm, is to recognize its importance. When I am teaching shooters, either individually or on one of my Positive Shooting courses, I try to make them more aware of rhythm. Many shots seem to have awareness of this aspect of shooting technique. One excellent way to develop good rhythm is to shoot in the company of really good shots as often as possible. Unconsciously, you will begin to adopt their timing. Visual discipline, balanced body position, good gunfit and trigger pulls, and a moderate-recoiling gun will also be aids to acquiring good timing. But, important though shooting with good shots – and the other things just mentioned – are, I believe that specific training is usually required too.

The majority of Sporting targets seem to be shot as if to three beats. However, it must be appreciated that the tempo will change from shot to shot. It is a function of the length of swing (which is determined by the angle of the target – a crossing shot will require a longer swing and slower tempo than a target which is quartering away immediately to the front), and the speed of the target. Tempo will also be affected by the distance through which the gun butt must travel: gun-up and gun-down styles require different tempos.

An excellent exercise to improve awareness of rhythm and tempo, which will also improve muzzle control, is to set up a crossing shot at medium distance (a Skeet range is ideal) and then to take the target at different points on its flight: very early, early, and late, as seems most comfortable. Timing should be modified according to each shot, but prolonged tracking on the late shots is to be avoided.

This exercise is best undertaken with a friend, who will tell you where to shoot before each bird is called, and who will tell you if you cheat! After a little while, move further away, or make the angle more difficult. Again, take the target early and late, and in what seems the most comfortable spot. Repeat the exercise

---

Coach's Checklist

As well as asking yourself 'How well does this shooter apply the Universals?', the following checklist may be useful to amateur coaches:

- Is the shooter's body aligned to the killing point for every shot?

- Is the shooter starting with the barrels of his gun pointed too far back or forward, or off the line of the bird?

   (Remember, however, that the 'correct' position will change depending on the speed of the target and the technique being employed to shoot it; a maintained-lead shooter starts in a completely different place to a Stanbury or Positive Shooting method shooter.)

- Is the shooter staying on the line of the bird during the mount? If not, why not?

- Is the shooter rushing or slashing at the target?

   One cause of this is mounting too early.

- Is the shooter trying to make sure of each target, i.e. failing to trust his initial instinctive aim?

- Is the shooter persistently behind the target? Why? Is body alignment or front hand position wrong? Or has the shooter failed to appreciate the concept of lead altogether?

- Is the shooter persistently shooting above or below the target? Why?

- Is the shooter moving his head on mounting, or lifting the head on firing?

- Is the shooter bringing the gun up to his face smoothly and pushing the shoulder into the gun? Or is he pulling the gun back into the shoulder and then cranking the neck down on to the stock?

- Is the shooter starting with the weight correctly distributed?

- Does the shooter look comfortable? If not, why?

- Is the shooter exaggerating body positions, thus creating tension and impeding swing?

- Is the shooter consistently missing down one side?

   (If it is the left side of the bird and the shooter is right-handed, suspect a left master eye.)

- Is the shooter following through?

- Does the shooter look confident?

- Is the shooter employing a routine?

- Does the shooter have any physical impediment?

---

using different starting positions: heel of butt below the nipple, just under the armpit and with the butt just out of the shoulder. Gradually you will become much more aware of the timing for each shot, and appreciate how much the starting position affects your rhythm. You will soon learn to identify the precise spot where each shot ought to be taken – 'the sweet spot' as John Bidwell calls it. The exercise may be repeated with birds overhead at moderate heights, and with pairs on report, which are a particularly good way of practising a graceful, flowing and well-timed shooting style.

This shooter is starting with his gun butt too low and his muzzles too high. Many game shooters tend to shoot like this when they first try clays.

Although the front hand position here is good, this shooter's head position looks a bit awkward; bringing the weight forward onto the front foot more could well be part of the answer; the gun stock might need shortening too.

This shooter's position looks a little strained. His front hand is too far forward, which could cause him to check his swing. However, one has to be very careful; some people achieve excellent results with unconventional positions. Ultimately the shooter must decide what suits him best.

This shooter has no relationship as yet between the muzzles of the gun and his line of sight. The instructor has spotted the problem and is about to correct him.

This shooter is having fun but she has mounted the gun on her upper arm and will not be able to control recoil effectively.

The muzzles of this gun appear to be a bit low. What will happen to the butt when the mount is completed?

Other Coaching Tips

Just telling someone they are behind or above a bird is not enough; you must tell them why they are, not just *where* they are.

- If someone has inexplicable difficulty in relating to a simple bird, a last resort is to get him to track its flight with his finger, then say 'Now just do the same thing with the gun'. Once he is on line, you can usually get him to kill it.

- Never encourage yourself or anyone else to shoot too much; it is always better to put more concentration into fewer birds.

- When coaching others or oneself, try to finish on success.

- If you get into real problems, have a break.

TRAINING AIDS AND EQUIPMENT

The first thing that might be mentioned, and which will be a boon to any keen shooter, is a portable clay trap and somewhere to use it. If you can arrange access to a field – you will need one which will allow for a 300-yard (300m) safety zone – you will find your own trap an extremely useful piece of equipment. It should be of the tripod or sledge type which can be sat upon; it should be powerful enough to throw good pairs and small enough to fit into the back of the car.

With your own trap and access to the land to use it, you and a friend can practise basic technique on simple birds, and you will also be able to work on the angles that give you particular trouble. It is amazing what can be done with a single trap and a little imagination.

Be aware, however, that traps are potentially

A portable clay trap is a useful investment for all dedicated Sporting shooters; you can split the cost with a friend or two. Of course, you must find somewhere suitable to use it.

dangerous. Never walk in front of a loaded trap. Always release a trap with thought to where your hand and arm are positioned. Make sure that you place the clays on the safe side of the trap. I have seen a lot of accidents with traps. Usually they involve arm injuries, but the really bad ones are when people get hit in the head by the trap arm or clay. Take care. Never get young children to trap for you. You have an obligation to instruct anyone else who traps for you in safe procedure. Finally, if you set up a trap in front of the shooting position, the trapper *must* have some sort of screened protection. This should not be a piece of ⅛in ply, but something that will stop a shot charge if it has to.

Video

Video is a marvellous aid to better shooting. As well as recording normal shooting sessions, you can make a record of your dry mounting technique. One may also make videos of friends and, most usefully, of top shooters in action. When using video, you should pay special attention to keeping the camera still when filming, and, if you are filming others candidly, without disturbing them. For coaching purposes, take some shots showing the upper part of the body and gun, others a little further back so that the feet, upper body and gun are visible. Faults in style show up very well on video; similarly, good style is usually very recognizable too.

Photography

Traditional still photography is a useful training aid as well, and Polaroid instant picture cameras are particularly useful. Everyone should study still photographs of himself shooting. As suggested with video, take some shots fairly close in, and others further back so that the feet and weight distribution may be seen clearly.

Mirrors

A wall-mounted mirror is also a useful aid to self-diagnosis. Is your mount smooth? Is your head staying still throughout the mount? Is there any 'snaking' of the muzzles as the gun comes up? Are the muzzles moving down during the mount and then coming back up to the line of the bird? Is your eye naturally aligned with the rib? Is your head canted on the comb?

Log Book

Every shooter who wants to improve should keep some sort of log book to record scores and observations about his shooting. Keeping a log book allows you to set training goals, and will make you more serious about your shooting. It is also a lot of fun. If you have a home computer, you may enjoy putting the information into that.

CONCLUSIONS

As long as you bear in mind the Universals of shooting, *visual contact, balance* and *rhythm*, diagnosis and fault correction are relatively simple. Amateur coaches following my system should aim to shape their students' behaviour to conform to the routine of the Four As (*see* Chapter 5, page 77). Keep drumming them into your students' heads.

8 Sporting Targets

PAIRS

So far in *Positive Shooting* we have barely considered the business of shooting pairs of targets. Let us set out some general principles to be applied whenever two targets are in the air simultaneously.

The first point to make is that there are always two separate targets to be assessed and shot – even when both birds seem to be moving in exactly the same direction. Treating both targets of a pair in the same way (as many are frequently tempted to do when both birds appear to be flying on the same line or are close together) may work sometimes, but it will never lead to the sort of consistent shooting that is our goal in Positive Shooting.

When you are faced with a pair at a clay shoot, the first thing to do, as always, is to watch very carefully. How different are the lines of the two birds? Does one drop off? Are they both travelling at the same speed? These are the important questions. As always, note the successes and errors of others – can you see why they are succeeding or going wrong?

Which bird should be shot first? For the sake of argument, let us imagine you are about to shoot a pair of simple crossers from a trap placed to your left. Normally, you would shoot the rear bird first, but set up your stance according to where you want to take the second shot.

So, let us imagine the routine. Set up your stance to favour the leading target. Now wind back towards the trap and bring the muzzles to rest at the point of first clear visual contact. Call for your targets. *Ignore the front bird* (which will take mental discipline as it comes into vision first), and instead, concentrate completely on the rear target. Shoot it first, then, ensuring that you are on the right line and, with a slight re-mount of the gun if necessary, move on to and through the front bird. Bang! Follow through.

Why do we usually shoot the rear bird first? It enables both targets to be shot in a single flowing motion: you do not have to move back and forth. Similarly, setting up the stance to favour the front bird aids smoothness as you do not 'run out' of body movement when you come to shoot the second target.

Exceptions

Although the rear-bird-first technique works in 80–90 per cent of situations involving simultaneous pairs, there are occasions when you may have to shoot the front clay first: most notably, when the first target dominates your vision in spite of good visual discipline or when leaving the first target would make the shot significantly harder (because it is dropping quickly or disappearing behind cover). When shooting 'the wrong way round,' set up the stance to favour the more difficult bird.

Pairs on Report

A pair on report from the same trap provides no special problems, as long as you return to the point of visual pick-up smoothly and quickly after the first shot. Too many shooters shoot the first bird well, but then try to intercept the second target with a stationary or nearly stationary gun.

Following Pairs

Following (or trailing) pairs, that is a pair released from the same trap neither simultaneously nor on report, but one immediately after the other, disconcert some shooters because they force a change in rhythm. As with pairs on report, the secret is to return to pick up the second target not only smoothly, but quickly. Usually the pick-up point will be substantially in front of the pick-up point for the first bird. Do not panic on these shots; you will probably have more time than you think.

Combinations on Report

Birds on report from traps placed in different positions can present special problems, particularly when each target requires a significantly different foot position. The general rule, assuming that it is not practical to change your foot position between shots (it often is), is to set up the foot position to favour the killing point of the more difficult target. If this makes the swing really awkward on the other target, you may have to compromise.

When you have shot the first bird, I would advise you to return immediately to a pre-selected pick-up point or zone for the second shot. The shots who succeed in competition on these mixed-report stands usually do so because they put more thought into preparation, and especially into stance and visual pick-up.

Simultaneous Release from Different Traps

This is a type of double which is encountered quite frequently in modern Sporting competition. It is fun, but can cause problems. The doubt from Station 4 at English Skeet is an example of this type of shot. Decide first which target to take first: usually, it will be the more awkward angle (because it is likely to get even more awkward if left). Then select your pick-up point for the first shot and a pick-up area or zone for the second. Next, consider stance. Usually, you should favour the second shot. When the time comes to shoot, take the first bird quickly but smoothly, with total concentration; when it breaks, shift your attention to the second target. Simultaneous combination birds are often hard only because of the unfamiliar rhythm. They are the sort of bird one should make a point of mastering.

Mixing Methods

Sometimes, when shooting at pairs, you may have to use a different shooting technique for each bird. Occasionally it will make sense to use a maintained lead or interception system on the first bird, to buy time to deal with the second.

SPECIFIC SPORTING TARGETS

If you master the Positive Shooting method, you will not need to worry a great deal about conscious lead when shooting most targets. Nevertheless, there will be exceptions: no rule is absolute as far as shooting technique is concerned. Even when one applies an unconscious forward allowance system, it is still desirable, when clay shooting, to make a conscious assessment of *every* target in the preparation phase (and indeed before, if you have the chance – the Army dictum 'Time spent in reconnaissance is never wasted' applies equally well to competitive shooting). For these reasons, I include here my observations on some of the more typical Sporting birds. The notes are written from the point of view of someone who applies lead deliberately.

High Birds

High birds are among the most satisfying of all to shoot. When shooters have problems with high birds it is often just a question of insuffi-

Canting the gun can be good technique if it helps to keep you on the line of the bird.

cient practice. There used to be a good excuse for this: until the recent boom in Sporting shooting only a few exclusive shooting schools could afford a high tower worthy of the name, hence few shooters had the opportunity to practise as much as they might have liked. Anyway, with all the high towers around today, there should be few excuses for missing. How does one cope with the bird sailing (or rocketing) above the treetops?

Go through the normal preparation phase. Establish the points of first clear contact and the approximate killing point: if the bird is driven straight overhead, this is likely to be just in front of perpendicular. A great mistake with high birds is to mount too early; with a high bird, especially one approaching from a great distance, you must slow down the tempo of the mount.

The muzzles should start from a position well up on the line of the bird. They may also be canted, if need be, to match the line of flight. This may sound like heresy to some, but when dealing with birds going out to one side or the other, a slight cant or tilt of the muzzles may help to keep them moving parallel with the bird's line of flight during the swing.

For birds driven straight overhead, no movement of the feet should be needed when the targets are coming in a predictable direction (and assuming you have set yourself up in a good position to begin with); be careful to keep the weight on the front foot (assuming a Stanbury or Positive Shooting method shooter), and to move smoothly from the hips. How to deal with high birds being presented at unpredictable angles is covered in more detail in the unpredictable targets section on page 102.

One must take care with straight-driven birds in two other respects. Do not be put off by swinging through and, temporarily, losing visual contact with the bird, in other words, *don't check the swing because you lose sight of the bird*. And, take the greatest care not to shoot 'up the side of the bird' because of insufficient concentration on line (when the line is really awkward, it may pay to treat a high-driven bird as a crosser).

Timing is especially crucial on all high birds; the shooter must develop the right rhythm: *one* on marking the target, *two* as the gun comes up and swings or strokes through, *three* as the trigger is pulled and the follow-through begun. Three beats, but to a fairly slow tempo.

Any other points worthy of mention? The commonest fault (even though high birds often appear further away than in fact they are) is to give them insufficient lead. Most people need consciously to make an extra allowance for high birds. Many shooters unfamiliar with these targets simply do not believe just how far in front they need to be to kill them. That does not mean that insufficient lead is everybody's error every time; another common mistake is to pay insufficient attention to, or be fooled by, the high bird's line.

The shot to the right seems occasionally to create special problems for over-and-under users. A number of right-handed, right master-eyed shots seem to have their attention distracted by the left eye during the mount and swing to the right when using this type of gun, especially if the gun has too much drop. It is a consequence of the over-and-under's high profile: the stacked barrels draw the attention of the left eye. The easiest cure – if poor gunfit is not the problem – is to close or squint the left eye.

High crossing and quartering targets may require a special effort to ensure you stay up on the line of the bird; strong arms and shoulders make them easier.

Grouse and Low-Driven Birds

Low-driven targets usually benefit from being shot with a fairly instinctive approach. All the basics apply: good visual pick-up, smooth mount, and follow-through; but with low approaching targets, everything will be happening at an accelerated pace. Because the gun is moving faster (or at least should be if the shooter is reacting well to the targets), lead is unlikely to be a great problem. Indeed, 'grouse,' especially those coming straight in or quartering only slightly, are one of the few targets which are often missed in front.

Because the targets are low, it is also easy to miss them above. However, with a low bird coming straight in, missing above and missing in front amount to the same thing; hence the old grouse shooting tip (which applies equally well to any low, driven clay target) of 'shooting them in the legs', or, for the more poetically inclined, 'Grouse wear spats'.

When presented with a simultaneous pair of targets, do not panic: you will have more time than you think. Poor shots slash at these targets; good shots demonstrate their muzzle control and economy of movement. Pick your first target carefully, glue your eyes to it until it is shot, then, and only then, consider the second shot.

Quartering Targets

The label 'quartering' target in fact covers a wide range of different birds which are neither crossing directly in front of, nor moving straight away from or towards the shooter. The quartering angles can be difficult to read; maximum effort to read the line correctly is one key to success.

Actually, following the line of some quartering birds with the gun can require special concentration, because sometimes there is a requirement to move smoothly in an unfamiliar direction, something which only comes with practice. Yet again I make the point that practice on birds that are unfamiliar is important.

The basic rule with quartering targets is to think about shooting the bird on the edge that corresponds to the direction of its line of flight. In other words, a clay or game bird quartering to the right should be shot on its right-hand edge, and a bird quartering to the left should be shot on its left-hand edge.

Quartering targets which look as if they are going more or less straight away or towards the shooter are often misread as straight, and the 'shoot 'em on the edge' principle works particularly well. Targets quartering away from or towards the shooter at extreme, almost crossing angles are often missed behind. The problem comes with the birds in between! These birds, at the middle angles, are frequently missed in front – especially when they are fast – and often over the top as well. The shooter over-estimates the amount of lead required, often failing to appreciate that the momentum of his gun will in itself give the bird sufficient lead. For most of us, there is no need *consciously* to see much, if any, daylight between muzzles and bird as the trigger is pulled, as long as the 'shoot 'em on the edge' principle is buried somewhere in our subconscious.

Woodcock

One bird which worries some Sporting shooters is the 'woodcock' stand. The greatest problems seem to arise when a woodcock stand is set up to throw a pair of targets quartering to the front of the shooter, but with a downward trajectory. Many will take the rear bird without undue problem, but will then swing through to the second which they miss behind and above. I find that missing above is common with many quartering birds and this problem is aggravated on a quartering bird with a horizontal or downward trajectory. So, when shooting a simultaneous pair of woodcock, the shooter often needs to shoot not just on the appropriate edge of the second bird, but to make a conscious effort to control the muzzles after the first shot to keep them underneath the second target.

Rabbits

Some shots seem to have inordinate difficulty with 'rabbits'. Clay bunnies are missed over the top, behind and, quite frequently, in front. A natural reluctance to swing a gun on a low line explains why rabbits are so often missed above; misses behind occur when their speed is underestimated; and misses in front occur when this target is rushed (which is not to say that one should go slowly with rabbits; generally, they are shot more consistently with a fairly rapid tempo).

I always make a point of shooting rabbits on the bottom edge, both because I have recognized the tendency to shoot over the top, and also because I know that if I go slightly too low the target is likely to break anyway. One has a slight leeway for error underneath, but none at all over the top.

When shooters miss rabbits behind, it is often because they are failing to react to them adequately. Poor reaction itself is often a consequence of poor preparation. Many times I observe shooters waiting for a rabbit with their muzzles pointing far too high or too close to the trap. If muzzles are too high, the shooter's vision of the clay is obstructed; if they start too close to the trap, it is likely that the shooter's eyes will not be looking in the right place for the first appearance of the target. The correct muzzle starting position for the Positive Shooter is just under the line of the target and out from the trap at the point of first clear visual contact. Body position is as crucial with rabbits as it is with any target, so make sure that you are aligned to your intended killing point before winding back.

Once you are set up, relax, put everything but the target out of your mind. I find that it generally pays to shoot rabbits quite quickly: an instinctive approach pays off with these targets. One rabbit target which is appearing more often in competition now is the quartering-away rabbit. My rule on these is, 'bottom front edge, not too quick and not too slow'. This can be a difficult target because the line is very awkward. Good preparation will make it easier, with plenty of control from the front hand.

Teal

Another bogy bird on clay shoots is the teal. Some people love them, but just as many start having negative thoughts when they see this target. There has been great argument on how to shoot teal, not least on the subject of whether they should be taken on the rise or not.

Teal tend to be missed over the top, beneath and often up one side or the other as well. This wide variety of ways to miss is often connected to inconsistencies in start position. The starting position of the gun is crucial with teal; it should be neither too high nor too low. Too high a start position will encourage shooting with a stationary gun (a common fault at teal) which will lead to misses below or above, the latter especially on targets which are moving up and away. Too low a start position can make a shooter slash through the target and miss above.

Select a start position which will allow you to come up immediately onto and above your first bird. I may sound like a cracked record, but you will be hard pressed to beat the Positive Shooting method's start: muzzles waiting at the point of first clear visual contact. An exception to this rule does occur, however, when the trap is not visible to the shooter. On these occasions, the muzzles should start where the shooter thinks he would first see the target if the trap were visible.

I always advocate shooting the first target as it rises, but not too early. Where should you shoot the second? My advice is, just before it begins to drop. Usually one will shoot almost *at* the second target; however, if the shot is mistimed, and the second target is at the very top of its trajectory, or beginning to fall, it will need to be shot with 'under allowance'.

Be particularly wary of the long-range teal quartering away. Here, I like to take both targets fairly quickly, with the gun starting almost

in the shoulder. I will shoot into the top edge of the first and the bottom edge of the second. If, on a pair of teal, one is faced with one target which is moving abruptly to one side, always shoot that target first.

Birds from Behind

I used to have a lot of trouble with high birds coming from behind. My problem was that I was not sufficiently familiar with this type of target – they felt alien to shoot. There are three tips for high overhead targets:

1. Make sure you know exactly where the other bird is coming from.
2. Look back to make visual contact as early as possible;
3. Allow your muzzles – which, unlike your eyes, should not be too far back – to travel with the bird for a while before they move in front or below it.

With overhead birds from behind, the eyes should be kept well up – considerably higher than the muzzles – to ensure early visual contact with the bird. The muzzles here are not as high as they appear because the bird is not being thrown straight out but at an upward angle.

When you fire, make sure you keep the gun moving. The vast majority of overhead targets are missed behind or above because the gun stops.

Droppers

One target which catches many people out is the long-distance dropper – that is, a target or pair of targets launched towards a shooter from high ground or a tower, which would land some distance in front of the shooter if not shot. Many mount too early on this target, track it and, much to their surprise, miss it cleanly even though it seems to be going quite slowly.

There are two ways to shoot droppers. Method one is with a very slow tempo, which allows the shooter to track the bird with the muzzles for some time, before mounting and pulling down. Method two is to snap shoot these targets at the last instant. I prefer method one for, although the targets look slow, they are deceptive and may require more allowance underneath or to one side than one might think. If you are having trouble with a dropper, try doubling your allowance underneath. I was at the Thornlands Shooting Centre in Devon recently where there was a particularly difficult dropper coming in from a fair distance and peaking very high. My friend and fellow instructor Ian Cawthorne saw that I was having a problem with the target and suggested that I try maintaining a six feet allowance underneath the bird.

Although I am not a conscious leader normally, I realized that was about double what I had been using before. It was good advice: next time I shot, the bird broke, and the time after that as well. Many shooters have the experience of suddenly realizing they have been misreading a particular bird, and it is most likely to be a target which is unfamiliar to them. Two morals: find someone you trust to tell you what you are doing, and shoot all the unfamiliar targets you can!

Loopers

Loopers are a rather artificial type of target which nevertheless are becoming more popular. They involve a trap set to throw a target in a distinct arc. Some like to shoot such targets very quickly to minimize the forward and under allowance necessary. I prefer to rely on timing. I enjoy shooting these targets to a reasonably slow tempo, being careful about allowance both forward and, crucially with loopers, underneath. For loopers, I usually need to see the lead picture consciously (remember there are no absolute rules on technique when one gets really serious about shooting – good technique is what works for you). I find that a conscious approach on this target usually produces more consistent results than anything else (there is an exception, however: a looping battue). Some shooters actually arc their swing to match the arc of the bird. The movement is from the waist. Try it; I will not say that it is wrong.

Battues

Battues are a wafer thin, flat, target which may be presented as loopers or as crossing or quartering targets. They are often a very challenging target because they are extremely fast, and because they tend to twist in the air in an often unpredictable or very awkward arc of flight. When I see a battue stand with lots of despondent faces, it usually means someone has tried to be a bit too clever and has set up a wholly unrealistic target. Treat it as a challenge nevertheless. When you face a very fast, wild target, go back to pure technique but accelerate your timing. Select killing and pick-up points carefully. Remember that a very fast target will require more lead.

Always shoot battues as quickly as you can whilst still being smooth. Silly battue stands showing simultaneous pairs are one of the few occasions when it may be tactically sensible to try to kill two birds with a single shot

This photograph shows why the edge-on battue can be such a hard target to break.

(normally, this is a very bad practice). Often the birds stay together till a certain point and then diverge wildly. Select your killing point just before the point of diversion if possible. But do not assume you will hit both with a single shot. Set yourself up to fire two shots.

Unpredictable Targets

Sometimes you will be required to shoot at unpredictable targets. Examples of this sort of shooting include flushes, walk-ups and events like 'Birdbrain'. Unpredictable targets fall into two categories: those which are slow enough to allow you to change your foot position (the majority) and those which are not. With both types of target, you must start in a compromise position, keeping your eyes above the muzzles, scanning the area where the targets may appear.

When you see your bird, if there is time to move, place the tip of the muzzles onto it and step into the bird's line, placing your feet towards the anticipated killing point. It is a

smooth motion with the front foot moving with the muzzles. On occasions when there is not time to do this, shoot the bird by relying on visual contact and upper body rotation. Both the situations considered are worth practising. A good way to do this is to use an auto-angling trap designed for Trap shooting. One may stand behind it and shoot various quartering birds (gun down, of course), one may stand to its side for a range of crossers and near crossers, and one may face it for driven targets. Ideally, in the latter case, it will be positioned behind a bank and elevated a bit.

General Advice

Think about your targets and watch others perform; if there is a stand where all the scores are low, study it. Where is the tendency to miss? Act on that intelligence. Be careful not to be fooled by a mixture of midi and standard targets – this seems to be a common combination these days in many Sporting competitions. The speeds, of course, are different.

Do not be afraid to use all the space in the cage or designated firing position to the best advantage; only stand in the middle if that is the best place to be (often it pays to get over to one side of the cage, or to its front). Although you may not be able to place your muzzles just where you want them, there is often the opportunity to turn your head and see the target and its line much earlier than would otherwise be the case. You must use your judgement; screwing the head around too much can put you off, but sometimes it offers a substantial advantage.

Finally, when shooting in or near woods, I often identify the spot on a tree trunk or branch where a target is first seen clearly, and which I will look towards as part of my shooting routine. This is especially useful when there is a distracting background. If you can eliminate the possibility of visual confusion by the application of a little common sense, do it!

This shooter is taking full advantage of the space available in the cage to set himself up.

Sporting shooters often have to contend with natural, but potentially confusing, backgrounds.

ENGLISH SKEET – SOME SIMPLE TIPS

English Skeet is fun in its own right and also excellent practice for Sporting Clays if shot with the gun down. Skeet offers an enjoyable and affordable way to improve many aspects of your shooting, including gun mounting technique, footwork, swing, visual discipline and mental stamina. Because it offers a good, but predictable, mix of easy to medium-hard targets on a compact layout, a Skeet ground is an excellent place to practise the principles of Positive Shooting (or, indeed, any other shooting technique). I often use Skeet to analyse my own and my students' Sporting technique. It is also one of the best places to start off a novice.

Before noting any specifics of how to shoot Skeet birds, we can say that these targets, like all others, are usually missed because of poor preparation and lack of concentration. None of the targets is that difficult on a Skeet layout, but they can all be missed if you have an undisciplined approach. As with any bird shot the Positive Shooting way, it is important that you establish where you first see the bird clearly, what its line is, and where you intend to kill it. On all the quartering and crossing targets (which is everything bar the straight-away birds on Stations 1 and 7) it is vitally important that you place your muzzles correctly – on the spot where you first see that target clearly, and just underneath its line.

Station 1 – High Bird

This bird is frequently missed over the top. When you take up position, make sure that you are immediately beneath the trap house 'mouth'. Your muzzles should be quite high – about 30 degrees to the ground. In this position they are ready to pick the bird up most effectively. It is a cardinal error with High 1 to position the muzzles low so that they have to come up to the bird. The correct mount for the high bird involves a pushing out motion as if trying to bayonet it in the sky.

There are a few people who tend to miss High 1 underneath because they 'slash' down through it or over-react to the bird. This is usually because their pick-up is wrong or because they are rushing. Once you have set up your gun position as described, look up slightly so that you can make early visual contact with the target. This will set you up to shoot the target quite quickly – before it gets to the centre peg. If all else fails (and it should not if you are practising what is preached in this book) try shooting six to nine inches underneath the high-house bird.

Station 1 – Low Bird

This target should present few problems. The only tip is not to be sloppy with your basic approach. Set the stance according to the killing point, which will be substantially to the left of the killing point for the high bird. When it comes to the double, set the stance to favour the second shot. This is a golden rule to remember with all Skeet doubles.

Station 2 – High Bird

This quartering bird is often missed over the top, and sometimes in front (especially when it has been allowed to pass the centre post). Make sure your stance is set to where you want to kill the bird, and that your weight is properly forward. Bring the muzzles back to the point where you first clearly see the target. Shoot it on the bottom right-hand edge quite quickly – before the centre post. You must trust your eye to direct the gun.

Shooters who allow this bird to 'beat them out of the trap' can miss the target behind. Having failed to react to the target initially, they then chase after it, but never quite catch up. The answer to that problem is not more lead but better pick-up. Many problems with forward allowance are actually problems of poor visual discipline – looking for the target in the wrong place.

Station 2 – Low Bird

This target should present few problems to a right-handed shot. If you are trying to teach someone Skeet, this is the target to start on (or High 6 for a left-hander).

Station 2 – Double

This pair causes problems for quite a lot of people because the rhythm of the two targets is very different. Set your stance to favour the second target, then really concentrate on the first shot.

Station 3 – High Single, Low Single

Station 3 presents no great difficulties for most people, although High 3 is easily missed over the top, especially if it is shot late.

Station 4 – Singles

These are often missed behind. If you are having problems and are satisfied that everything else is right (pick-up, stance, and so on), try a bit more lead. Theoretical lead is about 3in.

Station 4 – Double

Care and good timing are the keys to consistent success on this stand. As always, set the stance to favour the killing point for the second shot. It is particularly important on this stand to shoot the first target fairly quickly. The longer you leave it, the harder it becomes to shoot the second bird. Concentrate on the line of both targets. Ideally, you should shoot both birds on visual contact without conscious allowance. For some people, a more deliberate approach will be required. In either case, be very careful not to miss the second shot of the double over the top, or in front.

Station 5 – Singles

The high-house bird should not be a problem, but some people 'ride it down the range' in an attempt to make sure of it. This is poor technique and can lead to misses both behind and in front. Be careful not to shoot over the top of the low bird.

Station 6 – Singles

Again, the high-house bird should not present many difficulties, but the low bird does cause problems – not because it is a difficult bird, but because it is misread. This is a quartering target, and is often over-led. Shoot straight at it or, for some shooters, at the bottom left-hand corner. Speed of swing will take care of lead. Shoot it before the post.

Station 6 – Double

The double at Station 6 causes some people problems because they misread the low-house bird; a lot of shooters also make a mess of the relatively simple high-house bird. The reason is nearly always that they have set their stance for the first target. Because they are set up too far to the left, they run out of swing, rainbow off the line of the high bird and miss behind. Moral? Always set yourself up to favour the second shot.

Station 7

This is not a hard stand, but do not be lazy; many a straight has been lost by a 'take it for granted' attitude at 7. On the low bird, make sure your muzzles are well up and not much directed to the right – there is very little lateral movement required for the low bird. Just push into the bottom edge of the bird as if you were bayoneting it. As with every other stand, do not be sloppy with footwork on the double.

Other Tips

The best place to start a newcomer on Skeet is on the low-house bird on Station 2 for those who shoot from the right shoulder, and on the high-house bird at Station 6 for left shoulder shooters. Indeed these are excellent starting points for the aspiring Sporting shot as well. Learn to shoot singles first. Progress to doubles 'on report' rather than simultaneously released. Take pains to develop a good follow through technique. Bore holes into every target with your eyes. If you get into real problems on any bird, ask a really good Skeet shot to have a look at what you are doing (this is often easier to accomplish on a Skeet layout than at Sporting). Be cautious, however. When I say a *good* shot, I mean just that: a higher division A or AA shooter who has been involved in the discipline for some time. It is all too easy to get led astray by someone who does not really understand the problem. Advanced shots may also find it useful to learn to shoot Skeet with a maintained lead technique. There is much to be said for this method if one's primary interest is Skeet shooting.

Guns for Skeet

There are those who will tell you that you should shoot Skeet with open chokes and short-barrelled guns; the old standard was 26in barrels with wide-open chokes. Now the norm is 28in choked improved and improved, or improved and quarter. Some top English Skeet shots prefer a longer, steadier, 30in gun with a bit more choke. I use an even longer gun, choked ½ and ½, which may be too much, but it gives one confidence especially on Station 4. I also believe that guns for English and American Skeet should be quite heavy, both to help absorb recoil and to help with follow through.

9 The Psychology of Shooting

What is psychology? Simply, it is the science of the mind. It is a vast subject, and is split into sub-disciplines such as perceptual, cognitive, developmental, social and clinical psychology. There is also a relatively new subject area, much concerned with psychology, called sports science. Here, we need not worry too much about any formal boundaries. Instead, we can centre our attention on areas of knowledge that might be useful in understanding and improving shotgun marksmanship. Shooters will be especially interested in anything that might, (a) improve their ability to concentrate; (b) improve their 'motor' performance, i.e. their physical skills; or (c) help them cope with anxiety and match stress.

CONCENTRATION

Many competitors would argue that maintaining concentration is one of the most important skills in shooting; a momentary lapse can result in a missed target. The champion shot who has a good technique will find it easier to concentrate than the beginner. He is more in control, and less distracted because of a mastery of basic technique. He is not normally put off by thoughts about what he ought to be doing because he knows what he ought to be doing and usually does it. Thus the two basic rules for improving concentration are:

1. *Practise your shooting technique until it is as perfect as you can make it.*

2. *Know precisely what it is you need to concentrate upon.*

In the performance stage (the stage during which we call for the bird and shoot it), all our attention should be focused on the leading edge of the target. However, in the preparation phase before we call for the target, we must concentrate on selecting the pick-up and killing points and setting up a good stance.

How do we tell if we are concentrating or not? In the preparation phase, this is a relatively simple task for the Positive Shooter: if we break the Positive Shooting routine, we have probably broken our concentration. If we stick to the routine, we are, in all likelihood, concentrating. It is equally straightforward for a third party to assess concentration during the preparation stage by using the Positive Shooting routine (or something similar created for another technique) as their datum. Is the person shooting adhering to it? Has he aligned himself to the killing point? Did he wind the gun back to the point of first clear visual contact? Is he being sloppy?

As far as the performance stage – when we call for the target, shoot it and follow through – is concerned, the assessment of concentration is rather more complex. Shooting instructors, most of whom develop a feel for when students are concentrating or not, may suspect poor concentration whenever performance is erratic. Subjectively, most of us would surmise that we are not concentrating: (a) when we obviously feel distracted; (b) when we feel we have not focused our attention completely on what we

The focused concentration of these two shooters is self-evident.

are doing; and (c) when things are not going well. More objectively, we might note three indicators of concentration during the performance stage:

1. Reaction time to the target.
2. Physical response to the line of the target.
3. Eye focus (a variable which may well affect reaction time and response to the line of the bird as well).

Let us consider these a little more deeply. A competent shot who is concentrating will react well to the first appearance of the target (which does not mean that he rushes). The muzzles will have been well placed in preparation, ensuring that there will be minimum delay between seeing the target and moving the gun. A competent shot who is con-

centrating will also react well to the line of the bird. Without getting too involved in questions of shooting style, we might say that under most circumstances we would expect a competent shot using the Positive Shooting or Stanbury methods to move the muzzles on or just under the line of the bird. If they do not do this, we may conclude that they are either not concentrating, or that they are misreading the bird (or, in some circumstances, that they have a problem with the fit of their gun). Most importantly, the competent shot who is concentrating will maintain focus on the target (or better still, the leading edge of the target), from the point of first clear visual contact to the point when it is just a cloud of broken fragments. This sustained visual contact leads to a smoothness and decisiveness in the act of shooting which is very recognizable.

VISION AS A SKILL

As has been said repeatedly in this book, visual contact is the single most important factor in good shotgun marksmanship and it is also a very important index of concentration. Moreover, it is important to understand that seeing is not just a natural ability, it is a *skill* which must be learned. For example, we may have a natural ability to track moving targets: this is the foundation for learning how to see a target in the air, but we must overcome the equally natural tendency to release our focus from the object after a moment or two of watching it. The muscles of the eyes need to be trained, and a thought process needs to be created to manage and maximize our visual gifts. One way of improving visual awareness and discipline, is to memorize the image of the target we are looking for, thus creating a template in our mind's eye of what is correct. This will be a useful aid to visual concentration, which will give us a positive goal during the performance stage – simply looking for this correct image – and it will also help us to act whenever we see the wrong image.

To increase your target awareness, place a few clay birds (including non-standard targets) around the home or office. Photographs of clay targets, like the one used here to show the right image, may also be used. The idea comes from pistol shooting, where some serious marksmen place little stickers of 'Epsilon' – the letter E on its side, which corresponds to the correct sight picture in pistol shooting – around their homes on things like kettles, light switches and the like so as to heighten their awareness.

Improving Visual Concentration

In the early stages of learning to shoot a

To promote good visual contact, become intimately familiar with the shape of the target. I actually keep a few targets lying around the home and office for this purpose.

First-class shot John Rosenberg demonstrates the total concentration and controlled aggression that gets results. John is a film cameraman and I suspect that his critical eye for focus and his arm strength have been great assets to his shooting.

shotgun, our ability to maintain focus or concentration on the target is usually going to be dependent on good instruction and follow–up coaching, for example, someone telling us frequently to 'watch the bird'. As we get more experienced and start to really understand what we need to do to shoot well, we can take on the role of being our own coach: 'Well, I missed that one because I looked at the muzzles. This time I'm going to make sure I watch the front edge of the bird.' Even once we are visually aware, our focus and concentration may wander when we are tired – not to mention when we are distracted by noise, impaired vision, pain, the fear of failure or by

thinking too much about the mechanics of the shot as we are taking it. The effect of such circumstances is often to bring the focus back to the gun. The best way to overcome such potential problems is consciously to *lock focus* on to the leading edge of the target for every shot. Leaving it to the subconscious or 'instinct' is far too risky; it can fail for any of the reasons stated above and many more.

Sports Vision

In the United States, much more work has been done on the importance of eyes and shooting than in the UK. At least one book has been written on the subject (*see* below). A useful idea from this new science reiterates one of the basic ideas of Positive Shooting, but in a more technical language. Researchers talk of the peripheral visual field (what is around the target), the secondary zone (the target itself), and the primary zone (in our context, the leading edge of the target). In his book, *An Insight to Sports: Featuring Trapshooting and Golf*, Dr Wayne Martin maintains that optimum performance requires that all attention be focused on the primary zone during the performance stage:

Precise centering or zeroing in on the point of impact of any target is defined as completing the visual act. You must center precisely and lock tightly with your vision on the breaking point of the target. Yes, you must be aware of the total field, including the background of the moving target and its position through the peripheral field, but centred exactly on the strike zone . . . avoid any drift, shift, or in any way being drawn from the precise area of impact [head movement during the performance stage may cause this]. To smoke a target, one must center with pinpoint accuracy on the primary point of impact.

Eye Exercises

The Americans are particularly aware of the need to exercise the eyes. In his book, *Scherer on Skeet II* (*see* Further Reading), Champion Skeet shooter Ed Scherer suggests the following exercise every morning:

'Take a yardstick and hold it horizontally with your left hand in front of you. Holding your chin with the right hand to prevent head movement, try to look all the way to the left until you see the one-inch mark. Next, shift your eyes and try to see the 36-inch mark. Continue this exercise for five minutes each day, switching the yardstick to the vertical position half way through the exercise'.

I have another similar exercise to keep my eyes in trim. When I drive on the motorway, I focus on the number plates of the cars in front and try to keep my focus locked on to them for longer than would normally be comfortable. Occasionally, I will bring my focus back sharply, but briefly, on the speedometer, before throwing it forward again to lock on to another number-plate. Similarly, when sitting in a room and otherwise relaxing, I will keep changing focus from close objects to distant ones, and I will also follow the lines of the ceiling or the horizon for longer than is comfortable. You will be surprised at what hard work this can be; if you try it you will immediately become aware of the fact that your eyes are not only lenses, but muscles.

DEVELOPING A RHYTHM OF CONCENTRATION

We have considered some of the elements of concentration, and especially vision, but learning to see is not all there is to concentration. Even if we are skilled at maintaining visual contact, it is clear that we cannot concentrate all the time. To be able to concentrate on bird after bird, we need to develop some sort of strategy which allows us to rest between periods of peak concentration during the performance stage of shooting. Every shooter must find a *rhythm of concentration* which works for him and which can be applied even when he is not feeling 100 per cent physically or mentally fit. One famous Trap shot attributed his success to a simple system whereby he began to concentrate five seconds before each shot and allowed himself to relax five seconds after it. Many shooters align their cartridges before closing the gun. It is as if, having relaxed, they are focusing their energy on the gun before pushing it out towards the target.

As we have already seen, the Positive Shooting system uses a pre-planned programme of

111

This Trap shooter is clearly in the middle of a rhythm of concentration. He is oblivious to everything except the preparation for his own shot.

Many shooters find it useful to align their cartridges as part of their shooting ritual.

thoughts and actions. It will help you develop a rhythm of concentration. During the preparation phase of shooting, we are carefully considering the selection of killing and pick-up points according to the Positive Shooting routine. Once preparation is complete, our concentration shifts and focuses on only one thing: the target. During the performance stage of shooting, our concentration is at its most intense.

Focus–Fast

I suspect that many shooters do not realize how much effort should be put into every shot. Commitment must be total. I have experimented in recent years with a technique for Down the Line (DTL) instruction which combines many of the aspects of concentration that we have discussed so far. Many inexperienced DTL shooters have problems focusing on the bird consistently and tend to shoot too slowly – often because they have initially been slow to pick the bird up and then 'ride' it. The result is a miss over the top, and often behind as well on the sharper-angled targets. Having explained these things to a shooter so afflicted, and having shown them the correct muzzle start positions relative to the top edge of the trap house for the five shooting positions, I stand behind them as they prepare for the shot. Just before they shoot, I whisper 'Focus . . . (pause) . . . Fast'.

Results can be dramatic. There is often a sudden string of first barrel kills. However, with the average shot, it is usually not long before 'reinforcement' is required to maintain the new behaviour pattern which, in this context, is simply repeating the catch phrase with the correct emphasis. After prolonged reinforcement from the coach during a shooting session, the individual usually assimilates the new skill, but further reinforcement will be required from time to time to maintain the desired behaviour pattern. This applies to most newly learned skills.

Do not, however, misunderstand; I am in no way suggesting that 'Focus–Fast' is a cure-all. Far from it. It is no more than a simple way to help some average-ability shooters improve their performance at DTL. It works, when it does, because it communicates effectively three points to the shooter: to glue his eyes to the bird; to react to it immediately; and to have no hesitation in shooting, that is, not to 'ride' the target. It also makes him more disciplined in the way he shoots. With more experienced Trap shots, the technique is less likely to be successful because they should have already learnt these lessons. Nor does the technique work in Sporting shooting where the tendency of many is to rush. Nevertheless, my success with Focus–Fast has shown just how poor is the visual concentration of many shots. They have never been taught to *look* properly.

STRESS

Let us change direction a little now to consider stress and shooting. Some activities are more stressful than others. On a scale of 1 to 10, with deep sleep at 1, and being under fire in battle at 10, competitive shooting rates about 8½. In other words, it is a very stressful activity. Now I am not trying to put you off, because where there is no stress, there is little life; but it is important that we understand that our sport makes great demands upon us by its nature and that those demands are increased by our desire to do well and to maintain self- and peer-group esteem.

Although excessive muscular tension (one immediate effect of stress) can negatively affect our shooting, do not assume that stress of itself is an enemy. Stress, if properly understood and controlled, can be a very important ally. By assessing external stresses, our mind and body adopt the appropriate mode of response. For example, if we are driving fast or shooting, we shall need some extra adrenalin, oxygen and sugar in the bloodstream to perform at our peak; the body takes care of this automatically. Conversely, if we want to go to sleep, we do not want excess stimulants or muscle 'foods' in the bloodstream. Problems arise when our mind and body misread the external situation and over-react, preparing for battle rather than a mild punch up!

Shooters need to reduce excessive stress by developing the right mental attitude to their sport – quiet confidence with a sense of humour – and they need to become good 'stress managers'. As far as the latter skill is concerned, familiarity with high-stress situations will help; if you want to relax in competition, you need to shoot a lot of competitions, as well as being physically fit. But there are also some specific techniques which can help us to learn to deal with stress. One point worth making is that some people suffer more from stress than they need, because they have developed an obsessive attitude to their sport. It has become too important, too dominant in their lives and thinking. I believe that it is crucial that the individual who wishes to succeed in shooting, or in any other sport, maintains a sense of proportion. I see people every week who have become addicted to shooting. Those afflicted with the obsesssive or addictive mind-set cannot achieve their best until they conquer this psychological problem. The champion golfer, Nick Faldo, recently remarked that he thought his performance had improved recently because he now goes out to enjoy himself more than he did in the past, when winning was everything. The wisdom of that comment has always stuck in my mind.

The Inverted 'U'

Psychologists often talk of the inverted U relationship between arousal and performance. This suggests that up to a certain point, arousal improves performance, but there is a peak after which performance deteriorates because we are too stressed.

As a shooting instructor, I find that this sort of over-arousal tends to afflict quite a few male beginners. They are desperate to do well; their ego depends on it; but they rush and are very difficult to teach. With experienced shots, one often sees over-arousal leading to a desperate mental attitude; they must succeed at all costs. Their muscular tension increases as well and often their shooting goes to pieces. Over-arousal destroys their technique and, most notably, their timing. The Positive Shooter is in a

Shooters sometimes forget that they are involved in this game to enjoy themselves. Relaxing and having fun, when appropriate, is part of developing the right attitude.

Shooting is always exciting.

stronger and safer position, he has a routine to stick to and has a more conscious awareness of timing. However, anyone can become over-aroused on occasion. To cope with this one needs to be able to recognize it. My index of over-arousal in myself is feeling tension in my neck and shoulders; when this happens I consciously relax these muscles (*see* Exercise 2 on page 116) before continuing. If I were to shoot without doing this, the tension would inhibit free body movement and might well cause misses behind.

Meditation

Many international rifle and pistol marksmen practise meditation techniques to improve their ability both to relax and to concentrate. The demands of paper target and clay target shooting are different, but I think there is a place for active relaxation techniques in clay shooting, especially for those who find the stress of competition, or just shooting while being observed, a particular problem.

In meditation, one may be able to achieve a state of well-being by generating a mental image which one associates with tranquillity (for example, standing by a mountain stream; sitting in an empty room), or by fixing one's concentration on a sacred symbol or point in space, or simply by repeating a word or phrase. There are many different techniques and each individual must find the one that suits him. One

Four Relaxation Exercises

Here are four simple relaxation exercises. The first two might be performed almost anywhere. The third and fourth two are most suited to non-shooting situations:

Exercise 1 This exercise is derived from Yoga: slowly breathe in through the nose to a count of eight, hold for a count of eight, then exhale through the mouth to a count of eight. This sequence is then continued for several minutes.

Exercise 2 Working from the top of your head, let go of the tension from your temples, your eyes, your jaw, your neck, your shoulders and your stomach.

Exercise 3 Sit or lie down in a quiet place. Close your eyes and picture something peaceful, such as waves lapping a deserted beach. Breathe in and out deeply and slowly through your nose. Continue for ten minutes or more.

Exercise 4 Sit or lie down comfortably. Visualize your body. Now slowly go through it from bottom to top relaxing each part as you go. Start with your toes and feet, move up through your ankles and lower leg. Let go of the tension around your knees, relax the big muscles in your thighs and the area around your hips. Now relax the muscles in the lower abdomen, and through your stomach to your bottom. Take a deep breath, let go in the upper abdomen, and now the chest as well. Make your shoulders limp, feel the muscles soften in your biceps, in your forearm and in your fingers. Now focus on your neck, release the tension in the lower neck and up to the base of the skull, relax your face, part by part – jaw, ears, nose, eyes, forehead, scalp. Now you should be relaxed! Rest quietly for at least ten minutes.

When performing breathing exercises, one should always try to breath with the diaphragm rather than the chest.

Two Unusual Stress-Relief Methods

Biofeedback This is the process involved in a rather complicated, but intriguing, technique for learning to relax. It involves special electronic equipment which allows the individual to monitor bodily processes of which he would not normally be aware. Biofeedback equipment might monitor blood pressure, pulse, brain waves, stomach acidity or sweating. The readout from this equipment (a flashing light, meter-needle, or audible tone) combined with the conscious effort to modify the monitored response, enables one, with practice, to get a degree of conscious control over what are normally unconsciously regulated processes. Eventually the need for the equipment to achieve this will be replaced by the subject's greater awareness. Biofeedback may offer an accelerated means to learn how to relax; it certainly offers an interesting way to learn to relax. The most notable disadvantage is the expense and limited availability of the equipment.

Hypnosis The word comes from *hypno*, the ancient Greek for sleep. It is (usually) an artificially induced state of relaxation and concentration achieved by access to the subconscious mind. We are all familiar with the image of the man with the swinging watch, but there are all manner of other methods, including various forms of auto-hypnosis or suggestion where the individual acts on himself. I think all shooters need to learn how to think more positively, and there are many 're-laxation' tapes on offer to help shooters towards this end. The repetition of certain principles throughout this book might be considered a sort of hypnotic suggestion: **always watch the bird**.

secret of meditation is to let distracting thoughts float past; do not try to ignore them, just let them wander past like driftwood in a stream. Breathing techniques may also be used to induce peace of mind and a state of relaxed concentration – the *sine qua non* of good shooting.

THE X-FACTOR

With the rather detailed analysis of relaxation and concentration that we have made so far, it is as well to note that there is more to both than can easily be put into words. Brilliant shots seem to have the ability to 'throw' their concentration down the barrels, as if, after a period of preparation, they were projecting some sort of personal energy at the target. There is a smoothness to their movements as well. Whether watching a champion or a novice on a good day, an observer can often tell whether a target is going to break long before the shot is fired. What is it that rings a bell to say 'that's dead' long before the gun reaches the shoulder. My best guess is that this occurs when the movements of shooter and bird cannot be separated, or, more precisely, when they all seem part of the same whole. When the shooter is moving with the bird as if it were part of him, and without any glitch in the mount, the bird invariably breaks.

The ideas thrown up here are perhaps better understood in other cultures. In traditional Japanese archery, some unbelievable feats were carried out by grand masters; the literature talks of archer, moving arrow and target being one, or of the archer being the target. This is not mystical mumbo jumbo; many modern sportsmen and women have experienced that sort of feeling on occasion. Of course, what we need to learn is how to repeat it. The latest scientific research may help. Recent studies indicate that in both rifle shooting and karate, the successful shot or punch may be preceded by a certain pattern of brain waves. This is an important discovery as it suggests that one might be able to train sportsmen and women to produce that positive pattern before acting.

However, a simpler and more traditional way of increasing the proportion of right responses and learning to switch on the X-factor is good old-fashioned practice. During practice, when your performance is less than perfect, cast the memory of it from your mind; put all of your energy into what you *should* be doing; concentrate on remembering the feeling of doing it right. Shooting well is a skill which is learnt both by assimilating knowledge and by feel.

PRACTICE TECHNIQUES

Practice should always be structured towards well-defined goals. Seek out your bogy birds and work on them. Do not be afraid to miss birds in practice. When you have particular goals, you will find intense practice sessions can push you through barriers in a way that nothing else will, even though the benefits may take a while to become apparent. It is essential

If you want to succeed, you must develop confidence based on the knowledge that you have practised your technique to the point where it is as perfect as you can make it.

117

during such sessions that there is proper supervision – do not begrudge paying for it if you have to.

Make sure that your shooting technique is as well-rounded as it can be. Keep a log book. Always use the same routines in practice that you would in actual competition; every bird should be important, every time you shoot. I find it useful regularly to have small bets with shooting companions on the result of a round. It pushes me into a competition situation which is very useful. I also like, once every few months, to have several days of shooting at targets of medium difficulty under no pressure at all. I find this builds confidence. (Avoid targets that are too easy, though, as they will give you a false sense of confidence.)

Even when you deliberately shoot without pressure, never short-cut, or allow sloppiness to creep into your style. If you let yourself be sloppy, you are practising being sloppy and will therefore make sloppiness more likely in the future. Take pride in your style. The movements of the swing and mount should have a certain grace. This quest for elegance has very practical benefits when shooting in competition. If you are saying to yourself prior to a shot, 'I must mount as smoothly as I can on the line of the target,' you are unlikely to be saying 'I feel I am going to miss this one.' In other words, always emphasize to yourself what you *should* be doing rather than what you should not be doing. You may find it useful actually to say or think 'I *will* do x' before doing it.

Another general rule of practice is 'little and often'. Do not shoot yourself out. Whatever your ability level, feedback is vital. Often it will be impractical for you to be self-sufficient in this respect – hence the advice to find a coach you can trust, and to get your shooting videoed regularly. Keep an honest record of your performance. Plotting performance over time as a graph may also be useful. It is goal-oriented and creates a visible record of performance which may spur you on to greater things.

Visual Rehearsal

Although shooting a lot of cartridges is always going to be part of learning how to become a competent shot, it is also possible to practise usefully without expending any ammunition. One technique for doing this is visual rehearsal. Using it, one can go through a whole round of Skeet in the imagination, or focus on just one action such as the mount. If we rehearse something in our mind's eye before doing it, then our actual performance when we do it 'for real' is likely to be improved. Moreover, repetition of such exercises will of itself improve our powers of concentration. See if you have the discipline to shoot fifty Skeet birds in your mind's eye now. Could you manage a hundred? Try it. If you are an experienced competitive shot, as well as using this technique just to shoot birds, use it to see yourself winning. The generation of such positive images will actually make winning more likely because it helps to banish negative thinking. Some very serious shooters use the technique; they will generate an image of victory which even includes being awarded the cup or medal.

Dry Shooting, or Kata

Dry shooting should be a vital part of any training regimen. It helps to build up 'muscle memory' and concentration. I have devised certain dry practice drills for the Positive Shooting method, and I call them 'kata' after the set-piece exercise routines in karate. Similar exercises could be devised for any shooting style. Each kata is made up of a starting position, and three basic movements. Each movement should correspond to a beat, as in 'one – two – three.' Initially, the exercises should be performed slowly by numbers (spoken aloud); eventually, they should be practised more rhythmically with the movements and the words blending into each other. I have found that Kata 1 is also an excellent way to teach complete beginners to shoot: it allows 75 per cent of students to shoot gun-down from the first lesson.

Whenever you get the chance, pick up a gun and practise the kata. one — two — three.

Kata 1 – The Mount

Starting Position

Stand about six feet back from a wall upon which you have selected a spot just above head height – it should be imagined as a retreating target.

Your feet should be set up at one o'clock and three o'clock to the target (left-handers eleven and nine o'clock). The muzzles should be raised, the foresight a little below the line from your eye to the target; if the muzzles are too high – actually on the line – they will tend to chop down as you raise the butt.

The heel of the buttstock should be just below the level of the armpit. The sides of the buttstock should be very gently squeezed between forearm and rib-cage (the elbow of the arm in contact should be allowed to move naturally once the exercise begins). Your weight is predominantly on your front foot, but the rear heel is not yet raised.

The Movements

One Focus on the 'target'. The weight is brought slightly forward onto the ball of the front foot; the gun will come forward and the rear heel will naturally lift a fraction.

Two The gun is brought up with both hands and, simultaneously and smoothly, is pushed out towards the target as it pivots about the axis of the muzzles (it does not rise above the line of the bird). The rear heel and the right shoulder rise as one's centre of gravity and the gun are pushed further forward. (At the end of Movement Two, the gun should not be fully mounted, but halfway to the face and shoulder.)

Three The comb comes up to the face, and the shoulder pushes into the butt. The mount is completed.

Throughout the Kata, eye focus must remain on the imagined target. On completion of the exercise (assuming a reasonably well-fitted gun) the heel of the butt should be in line with, or just below, the top of shoulder. The sole of the butt should be resting somewhere between the collar bone and the shoulder joint and in firm contact with the pectoral muscle.

Other Kata

Kata 1 is a simple mount without lateral movement. Now devise your own kata for simple right and left crossers. Imagine the line of a bird. Select pick-up and killing points. Think about timing: one – two – three.

- **One** corresponds to the moment when the holding position breaks into movement on first visual pick-up.

- **Two** corresponds to the movement of the muzzles with the bird as the gun is raised towards face and shoulder.

- **Three** corresponds to the moment of firing and follow-through. I usually prolong the 'three' when I call out the beat: not 'one – two – three' so much as 'one – two – threeeeee'.

Kata – Conclusions

Experienced shots may devise kata for any bird. However, I would suggest that you devise a routine that is not too complicated, and that may easily be repeated. As an additional exercise, I recommend trying to perform your kata in slow motion, like someone performing the ancient Chinese art of tai chi. You will be surprised at just how difficult it is to mount the gun in slow motion. Slow-motion practice is good muscular exercise and will show up every small fault in your style. In the United States, a special sort of snap cap – the 'Trainer' – is available with a steel rod extension which allows the shooter to add weight to the gun for training purposes. These might well be useful in kata-type exercises. At the time of writing, I am experimenting with them.

Routine

With all clay shooting, discipline and routine are vital. Always go through the same procedures. If I were to use computer language, I should suggest you create a 'programme' in practice for your preparation and performance, and always run it when you shoot. The key is to create a programme that is flexible enough to cover the vast majority of situations, and that will not break down under pressure. You will be familiar with the Positive Shooting routine by now, but there is no reason why you should not create a programme for another method of shooting if you prefer. The essentials remain the same. Watch the bird carefully, note where it is coming from and select the 'killing point', create the stance according to it and wind back towards the trap, stopping at the pick-up point appropriate to the technique. Just discipline yourself to use the same sequence for every shot.

Maintain a Positive Approach

Sound technique builds confidence. If you know you have the ability consistently to break a target, your fear of failure will be reduced, and you are likely to break the target even when under great pressure. As we have seen, arousal and fear are interlinked. One can even fool oneself into thinking one is frightened just because one is excited. This happens because the mind would appear to say to itself 'Why am I aroused?' whenever the body is excited. If the context appears fearful to the mind (say if we have developed the wrong attitude to shoot-offs), we begin to feel fear. The key to coping with the fear of failure – which everyone suffers from to a greater or lesser extent – is to focus on success. If you behave and think positively, you will act positively.

The technique which I think works best, and which is one of the core ideas in Positive Shooting, is to occupy your mind before you shoot with the preparation for the perfect shot

Former World Champion, John Bidwell, a supremely confident shot, breaks two birds from the hip. John can break more birds from the hip than many shots can with the gun in the shoulder.

and the visualization of a perfect shot. Put total effort into every target and never consider your score until you have finished shooting.

One must do everything possible to develop confidence, but not arrogance. (I define arrogance as being mistaken in your perception of your own abilities.) True confidence is created by the observation of real success. To be a truly confident Sporting shot requires great technique, a positive approach and great experience of shooting under all sorts of conditions. I have often seen falsely confident shots turn up at shoots where the birds were unfamiliar, and then panic. The obvious answer is to try to shoot with as much variety as possible. There is a great deal of truth in the old saying that 'the best practice for competition is competition'.

If you restrict your shooting to club practice days, you cannot expect to do well in serious competition, because you will have neither the experience of match targets nor of dealing with the pressure at major events. Even with good preparation and the right mental attitude the shooter can get caught out by a particular target. In these circumstances rely on your technique and training to bring you through. Say to yourself, 'I will kill the target by preparing well and maintaining perfect visual contact.' When things get really difficult, the shot with a sound technique (or techniques) to fall back on is in a much stronger position than the person who 'just shoots them'. Whenever I experience inexplicable difficulty, I clear my mind and apply the Positive Shooting method precisely.

THE WILL TO WIN

Ultimately, to win, you will need more than just a good style and regular competition practice; you will have to want to win. It has been said that few really rich men win the big prizes because they are not 'hungry' enough. Learning to relax is important to good shooting, but so is being able to turn on *controlled* aggression when necessary. Try doing this sometime when you are shooting.

Learn to use your competition nerves positively (remember, everyone else is nervous as well), and see them as an aid to your reaction time. Never say to yourself, 'Stop being nervous'; it will make it worse. Rather say, 'Go on, be as nervous as you like,' and then project that

This disabled shot, acting as a student on an instructor's course is, in fact, a first-class performer. Many disabled shooters compete on equal terms because they have the determination to succeed.

energy at the targets. As we have already noted, every shot must be given 100 per cent concentration, ignoring all distractions. British Olympic pistol shooters have been subjected to Klaxons and other noise makers during their training shoots to make them as impervious to distraction as possible. If, in spite of the application of good technique, you find you have been distracted, for example by a 'no bird', stop. Break the gun, and go back to the beginning of your shooting routine and start again. Don't be lazy, and never allow yourself to be hurried.

When I am distracted, I like to think of it as a challenge: 'This thing may have broken through my concentration, but I am going to prove to myself that good technique can still kill that target.' Every time I do that, the next distraction is a little easier to deal with. Since

---

Shoot-offs

If you want to get to the winner's rostrum, learn how to cope with shoot-offs. Many experienced shots like to shoot first in these situations to put the other man under pressure. As with all shooting, take it target by target, and forget your score until after the shooting has finished. Shoot-offs often involve very difficult targets and can be won on low scores. Avoid talking to others as there is the chance that they may say something that will put you off (perhaps deliberately).

---

any interruption or distraction tends to bring your concentration back to you and away from the bird, remember that the thing that is most

Whether it is a village shoot or the British Open, winning is always a pleasure, but the Sporting shot wants to be a good loser too. He should take pleasure in shooting well; if he is in the prizes occasionally, it is an added bonus.

easily lost in such circumstances is visual contact.

Psychological Warfare

On occasion, you may find yourself pitted against someone who is deliberately trying to put you off. This might take the form of a single remark, or a sustained effort to disconcert you by an aggressive manner, or by such things as talking on the firing point or poor buttoning. There are even instances of people deliberately trying to put others off by shooting to an abnormal rhythm. Expect the unexpected, then it will not disturb you. You must also remember that you are a victim only if you allow yourself to become one. The best initial response to a deliberate attempt to put you off is amusement. This will keep you in the right frame of mind, and may, incidentally, have the effect of making the gesture rebound. You might even exclaim with a smile, 'You're not trying to put me off by any chance,' to the perpetrator. If the situation persists, remind yourself that whoever is doing this to you is doing it for a reason; *you are a threat*. He fears you, and the possibility that you will win.

I will end this section on psychology on two thoughts:

- Improvement in performance is dependent upon intelligent self-observation. Watching ourselves is not enough. We must be able to understand what we are doing, if we are to improve.
- Physical and mental processes are part of the same whole. As you build a routine for yourself, make sure that it contains both elements.

PHYSICAL FITNESS

If you are determined to become a first-class shotgun marksman, it will be a great help if you are physically fit. Quite aside from the physical benefits that getting into shape can bring, the effect that it can have on the mind must not be underestimated. The shooter who is fit will enjoy a sense of well-being that will promote self-confidence and improve concentration; and the effort required to stay fit will also help to develop self-discipline, which, as we have seen, is one of the most important factors in improving shotgun marksmanship.

We may identify two types of fitness as important to our sport: cardio-vascular (heart) fitness, which affects stamina, concentration and general health, and the fitness of the specific muscle groups involved in mounting the gun and providing a stable gun platform. You may address both types of fitness with different exercises, or you may opt for those exercises that improve both simultaneously.

Getting Fit

Swimming is an almost perfect and unstraining exercise for shooting because it helps us with sport-specific fitness (toning arm, shoulder and leg muscles), it promotes suppleness, and it provides us with cardio-vascular exercise. I always recommend swimming first, because it is such an enjoyable form of exercise for most people; injuries are uncommon and it is easy to develop a routine. Tennis can also be an enjoyable form of exercise, and is useful 'cross-training' because eye–ball contact is so important (the Positive Shooting triangle of Universals would apply well to tennis: not only visual contact, but balance and rhythm are all required to play well).

If you prefer to jog, run or play other ball games, do so by all means – whatever you enjoy and will persist at. Rowing and cycling are excellent, even walking if you push yourself to go a little faster than normal. If you want to be less traditional, aerobics are a brilliant way to get very fit quickly. One of the best ideas I have heard of (from an RAF officer who is a top pistol shot) is to put an exercise bike in

Many Sporting shots have very powerful upper bodies. Look at the strength in this man's forearms. Also note his evident determination.

front of the television and make a contract with oneself to pedal through the evening news each night! Whatever sort of exercise you opt for, to benefit from fitness training you should exercise several times a week for at least twenty minutes. You will find it much easier to persist in such exercise regimens if you work out with a friend on a regular basis.

Pumping Iron?

Although good muscle tone is essential to shoot really well (look at the arms and shoulders of the best shots), I do not recommend serious weight-lifting for shooters. It is time consuming and conducive to injury; moreover, mas-

sive muscle bulk is an impediment to good mounting and may also disturb timing. However, many international-class shots have proved that circuit training with light weights can be very useful. My own exercise routine consists of walking whenever possible (no buses or lifts), swimming twice a week, morning press-ups and sit-ups, and a nightly kata session as described earlier. In the summer, I row and play tennis as well.

Precautions

If you are over thirty-five, it is sensible to see your doctor before starting a programme of regular exercise, or at any age if you have had chest pains, high blood pressure, asthma, bronchitis, diabetes, or back or joint trouble (or indeed any other serious health problems). Do not exercise when you are feeling unwell, and stop exercising when you feel pain or dizziness, or when you feel sick or unusually tired. Build up your fitness gradually, preferably with a friend or family member. Always warm up before vigorous exercise, and put aside a little time after exercise to cool down. Most injuries are the result of the overuse of joints and muscles.

Warming Up

Improving physical condition makes sense to any sportsman, but fitness training is not all there is to the story; we must understand how to make best use of our bodies. Warming up, in particular, is vital before any physical training to avoid injury, and it is also important before we shoot so that lack of suppleness does not impede the mount and swing. My own pre-shooting warm up includes stretching the arms out and yawning, opening and closing the grip of the hand quickly (fifty times), rotating from the hips with hands on hips bringing the elbows forward alternately (twenty times), rotation from the hips with the arms held forward as if sleep-walking (twenty times), forward bends from the hip with hands on hips (ten times), toe, or near toe touches (ten times), slow chin/neck rotations (ten times). I finish this routine with a breathing exercise and a relaxation exercise as described earlier (Exercises 1 and 2 on page 116).

Food and Fitness

A balanced diet is important to our general health, and crucial when we are trying to get fit. Most of us will be familiar with the recommendations to eat more fibre (fresh fruit, vegetables, whole-wheat bread) and less saturated animal fat. None of this need be that painful: grill food rather than fry it; have an apple or

orange instead of a bar of chocolate; seek out fat-free or fat-reduced products. As well as eating too much animal fat, most of us consume far more sugar and salt than we need. Sugar has almost no nutritional value, it is often used as a means to make processed food taste better; why not avoid it? Excessive salt should be avoided because it can increase blood pressure.

Ideally, one wants to be just a little hungry before exercising or shooting. Being a little hungry stimulates us to be a little more alert, better prepared for physical activity; conversely, excessive food intake tends to make us switch off physically and mentally. If you need a snack while shooting, nothing is better than an apple or a banana. As far as drinks are concerned, Trap champion Kevin Gill tells me the ultimate 'isotonic' boost is water and apple juice.

Weight Problems

Although some heavy people are very good shots, they could improve their stamina and long-term chances of survival by losing weight. My own experience, as someone who has frequently battled with his weight, is that exercise is more effective than dieting as a means to weight reduction; but both require will power. One simple diet that does work is the 'fat-free' system, where any food that is obviously fatty is eliminated from the daily intake.

Tobacco and Alcohol

I doubt if there is anyone left in the world who is not aware that smoking and drinking to excess are bad for health. Smokers have more than twice the chance of having a heart attack than non-smokers, and an increased chance of lung cancer. Nicotine makes the heart beat faster and raises blood pressure. The carbon monoxide in cigarette smoke reduces the oxygen in the blood and makes the heart work harder. The tar in tobacco damages the lungs. The downside of alcohol (which in small quantities can be beneficial) is no less worrying.

Heavy drinking can lead to heart disease, brain damage, liver dysfunction, ulcers, impotence, alcoholism and, not least, hangovers.

One should never drink and shoot, just as one should never drink and drive. Even modest quantities of alcohol will damage the fine co-ordination skills upon which safe shooting is dependent. Although I enjoy cigars, wine and beer, the evidence is now indisputable: tobacco smoking of any sort and alcohol in excess (more than about two pints of beer a day or its equivalent) will damage your health. If you have the discipline to moderate your consumption, you will be applying the very same strength of will you need to succeed at shooting. It will not be easy, but it is certainly worth the effort.

Clothes and Equipment

Do not waste money on designer clothing and expensive equipment for fitness training. A pair of small weights may be justifiable, and perhaps an exercise bike. There are always a few of the latter for sale cheaply in the local paper — witness to the determination required to keep fit. All sorts of fitness equipment can be acquired easily and very cheaply second-hand; all things considered, it makes little sense to buy it new. If you want to take up walking or running, good shoes are a justifiable expense. Shoes that have inadequate side support, or an inadequately cushioned sole, may cause damage to your joints and back.

10 Gunfit

I have tried not to make this book too equipment oriented. In shooting, everyone has an excuse when things do not go well, and one of the most common is that the gun is not right in some way. The Positive Shooter will be able to shoot competently with less than perfect equipment. This said, I do believe that equipment selection and modification are important, especially gunfit. A well-fitted gun – one which requires minimum adaptation of the body to the gun, which controls recoil effectively, and which naturally shoots towards or just above where the shooter is looking – will make it easier to shoot well, particularly when we are tried or off form. Most top-ranking shooters are very fussy about the fit of their guns. I certainly know of many cases where the shooting performance of an individual has been transformed by the acquisition of a well-fitted gun.

The shooter who wants his gun fitted has a choice. The obvious option is to visit a professional fitter with a good reputation; the second is to attempt to fit himself. Although it has potential pitfalls (Robert Churchill likened it to self-doctoring), there is something to be said for do-it-yourself gunfitting. Not only is it cheap, but, as long as a methodical and cautious approach is maintained, there is much that the shooter can learn about himself and his gun.

THE BASIC VARIABLES

Gunfitting involves the manipulation of stock measurements; it may involve a change in the stock design as well. The basic variables of gunfit are length, cast, drop (also known as bend) and pitch.

Length

The length of a gun stock is the distance from the centre of the trigger (the front trigger with

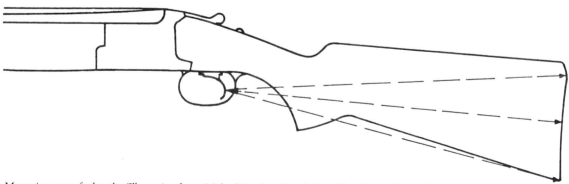

Measuring a gun for length. (Illustration from: Michael Yardley, Gunfitting: The Quest for Perfection, *Sportsman's Press, 1993).*

Stock fit on this gun looks about right. Notice the gap between the nose and the base of the thumb and the position of the heel at the shoulder.

double-trigger guns) to the centre (sometimes called the middle) of the butt. Typically it is about 14⅜in on single-triggered over-and-unders. An expert gunfitter will also measure the length from the centre of the trigger to the heel/bump of the butt and from the centre of the trigger to the toe of the butt, as well as the length from centre to centre. The length to heel/bump and toe will affect the pitch of the gun, which will be considered shortly.

The simple rule for length is that the shooter should have as long a gun stock as he can comfortably and consistently mount. Too long a stock may check the swing. Too short a stock may reduce control and increase felt recoil. The right stock length may only be ascertained precisely by shooting at targets. The popular

method for checking stock length mentioned in Chapter 3 – holding the gun at the grip and seeing if the rear of the butt makes contact with the lower bicep when the arm is bent at 90 degrees – should not be considered as more than a very rough guide.

Cast

The cast of a gun is the amount the stock is set over to the right or the left in relation to the rib of the gun. Cast is measured 'at heel', and also, by the professionals, 'at face', 'at comb' (which means at the front of the comb), and 'at toe'. A stock angled to the right, is referred to as having 'cast-off' and a stock angled to the left is referred to as having 'cast-on'. Most mass-

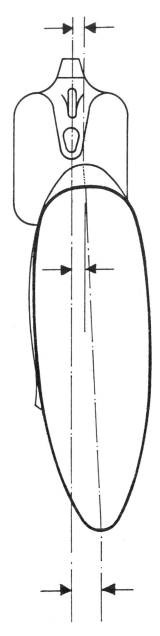

Measuring cast: at the front of the comb, at the heel of the stock, and at the toe of the stock. (Illustration from: Michael Yardley, Gunfitting: The Quest for Perfection, *Sportsman's Press, 1993.)*

produced over-and-unders made with cast will have about ⅛in of cast at heel and ³⁄₁₆in or ¼in of cast at toe. The basic principle with cast is to create a gun which when mounted will, without adjustment of the head, place the shooter's master eye in line with the rib. Traditionally, right-handers (with right master eyes) will want some cast-off and left-handers (with left master eyes) some cast-on, while broad-shouldered people will usually want more cast than the slightly built.

I work to the principle that cast should be kept to a minimum, especially on over-and-unders. The point of impact of these guns can react unpredictably to extremes of cast. Extremes of cast also increase felt recoil. Some competitors are now reconsidering the merits of the so-called offset comb, a comb in which the deviation from the line of the rib is constant, or nearly constant, from front to rear. The offset comb has the advantage that recoil is directed in a straighter line in the horizontal plane, and that cast at face may be achieved without moving the heel of the butt out excessively.

Drop

The drop (or bend) of the gun is the vertical distance from the top edge of the stock to the top of the sighting rib (a gun must have some drop, or the muzzle of the gun would always come up above the point of aim). Drop is usually measured 'at comb' and 'at heel'; typical measurements would be 1½in at comb and 2⅛ in at heel, but what really counts is the drop-to-face, because it is this which establishes the critical eye–barrel relationship. For Sporting shooting, the drop should usually be adjusted so that the gun will pattern about 60 per cent above the point of aim (although some shooters prefer a slightly flatter shooting gun, and a few a higher shooting gun). I always bear in mind, when fitting for drop, that a great many Sporting targets are missed over the top.

To see if the drop is approximately correct, a professional fitter will – having proven the gun

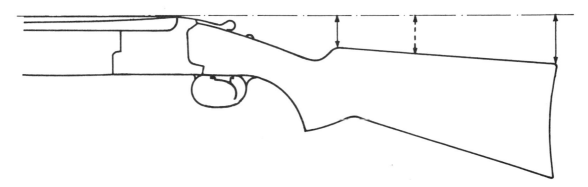

Measuring a gun for drop. The crucial measurement is at the point where the stock and face touch. (Illustration from: Michael Yardley, Gunfitting: The Quest for Perfection, Sportsman's Press, 1993.)

clear to his own and his client's satisfaction – look at the client's eye–rib relationship from the muzzle end of the gun (when practised by professionals, the procedure is safe, even though I acknowledge that it breaks the golden rule of gun safety). Most fitters like to see the pupil of the eye just above the rib, but some like to see the iris sitting on the rib. What really

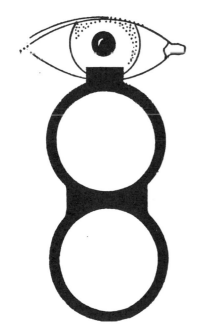

The position of the eye above rib/breech is a matter for some debate. The eye on the right is almost certainly too low, but much depends on the regulation of the gun. (Illustration from: Michael Yardley, Gunfitting: The Quest for Perfection, Sportsman's Press, 1993.)

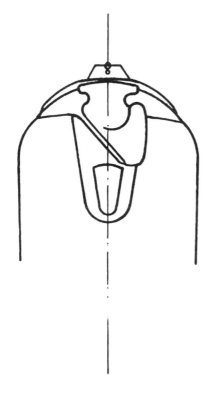

The classic figure 8 relationship between two sighting beads. On a Sporter, I like to see a fraction less rib, but much will depend on the individual regulation of the gun. (Illustration from: Michael Yardley, Gunfitting: The Quest for Perfection, *Sportsman's Press, 1993).*

counts is how the gun actually shoots; different guns, with different barrel regulation can have widely differing points of impact, regardless of where the eye appears to be in relation to the rib.

As well as controlling the eye–rib relationship, drop and cast affect the placement of the butt at the shoulder. There is much talk of fitting guns to the so called 'shoulder pocket' (the area between collar bone and shoulder joint, which you may feel if you fold your arms in front of you and then move one hand up). Many people will indeed want their gun fitted to nestle in the shoulder pocket, but some, including those with narrow shoulders and those who tend to stand edge on to the target, will mount their gun a little further out, almost on

the shoulder joint. What is definitely wrong is to mount the gun on the upper arm, or to have the toe of the gun butt positioned under the armpit. The gun must be comfortable and positively located. The top of the comb should be in line or a fraction below the top line of the shoulder for the majority, though there are some who will only be comfortable with the butt position lower.

Shooters can adapt fairly easily to a gun that is too short or long, or wrongly cast; making do with the wrong drop is far more difficult. Many guns coming in from the Continent and the United States often have far too much drop for effective Sporting use. Some are also afflicted with steeply sloping combs; the problem with such stocks is that during recoil the front part of the comb will tend to come back and bash the shooter in the face. Stocks with parallel stock-combs (where the drop at comb and heel is the same or nearly the same) are worth serious consideration for these reasons: they reduce felt recoil and they promote consistent mounting because a slight error in head position will have less vertical effect than with an inclined comb. It is often possible to modify a gun stock to reduce the incline of the comb; it may be bent up and the comb recut if necessary, or, if the butt placement at shoulder is about right but the drop at face too great, a piece of wood may be added to the top of the comb and finished to the required specification. I always try to keep the difference between drop at comb and heel below ¾in on a conventional stock; if the client requires more, a Monte Carlo stock or something similar is needed.

Pitch

Another important gunfitting variable is pitch, which is often (but imprecisely) measured by placing the butt on the floor next to a vertical post or wall. With the top of the action touching the post or wall, any variation from the perpendicular can be measured. Pitch, which is controlled by the length of stock to bump and

Andrew Perkins of Holland & Holland takes measurements off a traditional try gun.

toe, is nearly always downwards. With an over-and-under set up for Sporting Clays, a normal pitch-down measurement would be about 2½–3in. Pitch affects the way the gun is mounted, and may have a subtle effect on the vertical placement of shot. When fitting, I try to create a gun where neither the toe nor the heel come to the shoulder first, and where the shooter's shoulder is in good contact with the butt sole throughout its length. Pitch and butt-sole shape will, of course, affect the way recoil is transmitted to the shoulder.

Grips

Grip shape and size are important gunfitting variables which do not get as much attention as they deserve. A grip should obviously fit the hand; many do not. Someone with stubby fingers will probably want a shorter grip than someone with long fingers. It is also important that the angle of the grip is comfortable and does not cause you to cock the wrist either up or down. A good grip shape, balanced with a good fore-end shape will encourage both hands to work together. Grips may be reshaped by a competent stocker, who may thin a full pistol grip, remove a palm swell, or change the pattern of the grip; full pistol to semi-pistol is a popular conversion. The stocker might remove a little wood from the nose of the comb or change the flutes to each side of it to make the gun more comfortable for the user. He might also change the side profile of a grip so that it is diamond-shaped rather than round.

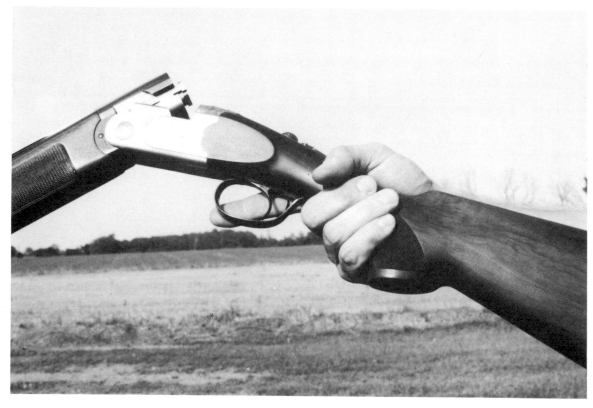

Grip shape and size is vital. This grip looks too short for this hand.

Many Continental guns seem to have badly designed grips. Often, they are too full, and have usually been designed for Trap shooting where the gun is pulled back into the shoulder. In Sporting shooting, in the classic styles, the gun is pushed out toward the target. This is easier to do when the grip is not too sharply angled. A good grip design should not be much deeper at its rear than it is at the front. Grips that become much thinner towards their front are hard to grasp in recoil. I think a fairly thick semi-pistol is the ideal Sporting shape. Some full-pistols are very good, but many encourage the rear hand to act independently, which is a bad thing. Straight grips are not often seen on Sporters, probably because they offer poor muzzle control. The semi-pistol grip is a good compromise.

Fore-ends

Fore-end and grip should complement one another. I do not like to see a fore-end that is too thick or too narrow on a Sporter. Schnabel fore-ends look pretty (sometimes, anyway) but I think the most sensible pattern of fore-end is something like the one seen on the Ruger Red Label guns; the parallel-sided Beretta Trap fore-end used on 682s is excellent too.

GUNFITTING PROCEDURE

Before you can usefully check the fit of a gun, you will need to know which is your dominant eye; you will also need to be a reasonably competent shot. There is little point in someone who has not learned to mount the gun bothering too much about gunfit. Assuming that you know which is your master eye, and that you are a reasonably competent shot (unless you have been shooting for two seasons I would not attempt any of this), you will need your gun, and somewhere to set up a pattern board. If you have access to a proper pattern plate, so much the better. The pattern board need be no more than a large sheet of brown wrapping paper on a wooden frame. It is very important, however, that you ensure that there is either a solid backstop (such as an earth bank) or a 300-yard (300m) safety zone behind your board.

Set the board up so that its centre is at eye level, and give it a clear aiming mark (not a pencil cross). Fit the tightest chokes you have and retreat to sixteen yards. (At this range a ⅛in adjustment to the stock should have a 2in effect at the target.) Without being too hasty or too deliberate, lock your eyes onto the mark and shoot at it, starting from a normal, unexaggerated, gun-down position. Note the centre of impact and repeat the procedure about half-a-dozen times. Where is the mean point of impact building up? Ignore any wild or mismounted shots. Do the same for the other barrels of a double gun, keeping a record of which sheet corresponds to which barrel. If results are still inconsistent, you can try shooting gun up.

As well as shooting at plates, you will want to shoot at targets, preferably with an

Perfect shot placement for a Sporter: very slightly high. The pattern itself appears to have a few holes in it.

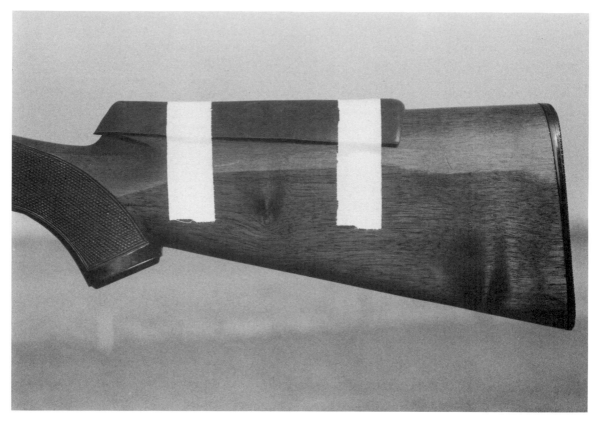

A detachable comb-raiser.

accomplice who can see shot (the trick to this is to stand just to the side of the muzzles and throw your vision out to a point about twenty feet (6m) in front). Overhead birds and fast, close, and mid-range crossers are good for assessing stock length. Straight going-away targets, and medium-high driven birds are very good for cast. Drop may also be assessed on straight going-away birds, and on crossing and quartering targets as well. A long, fairly high target travelling at medium speed is especially useful for this purpose.

If your gun shoots consistently high, low, left or right, it may need to be altered. You may well be able to undertake some trials in the field. If your problem is low shooting on everything, it may well be worth trying to build up the comb. There are all sorts of ways of doing this, using a rubber comb-raiser, strips of cardboard or plasticine covered with tape, moleskin with cardboard underneath, take your pick. You might even consider a gun with an adjustable comb, although I would not generally recommend them for Sporting use. (If you do opt for one, have the sharp edges of the comb section rounded off, otherwise they will cause a glitch in mounting. I also suggest you get a comb adjustable for different heights at front and rear, and which has a variable cast capability – the best in the UK is made by Allen Rhone, *see* Useful Addresses.) When you build up comb height, do it in small increments.

If the problem is high shooting, caused by too high a comb rather than too long a stock,

Some people do extraordinary things to their guns in the name of gunfit.

you will not be able to do much in the field. No matter, take the pattern sheets to a gunsmith and explain the problem or, if you are a competent woodworker, reduce the comb height yourself by carefully removing wood with a rasp or file. If you do this, be cautious in how much wood you remove, use a straight edge occasionally to make sure the top of the comb stays flat, and also ensure that you do not change the shape of the comb excessively. When you have got the gun placing its pattern where you want, you can fine-finish the modified butt with emery paper and rub in some linseed oil to complete the job.

If you have difficulty in mounting the gun because it is too long, you may be able to deal with the problem temporarily by removing a recoil pad or butt plate. If the stock is too short, you can lengthen it for trial with a rubber or leather butt extender. Pitch may be adjusted by loosening the screws of a recoil pad or butt plate and packing one end or the other with card or coins.

Regulation

The most awkward problem you can discover is that the barrels are improperly regulated. If you suspect this, give the gun to a skilled barrel maker for an opinion. It is my experience that many over-and-unders shoot too high with the top barrel relative to the point of impact of the bottom barrel. The discharge of the top barrel tends to cause more rotation at the shoulder

While this shooter's stance is good, the stock is too long; she also appears to be raising her head slightly.

because of its higher position relative to the shoulder. (If you have difficulty understanding this, imagine the effect of having a top barrel a foot above the bottom barrel: the higher its position, the more rotation one can expect).

Over-and-unders intended for Sporting use should all be regulated so that both barrels fire into each other. If your gun does not do this, it may be possible to have it re-regulated or, if the problem is minor, elect to shoot the top barrel first (an excellent remedy for some Trap shooters where a high-shooting first barrel and a flat-shooting second barrel may be just what they need). Another option is to acquire a gun that allows for adjustments in regulation at the muzzles; yet another is to acquire a single-barrelled repeater. I think manufacturers might explore more fully the physics of the over-and-under and its interaction with the user. Barrels that are mechanically true will not necessarily shoot to the same point of impact when the human user is added into the equation.

CONCLUSIONS

It would be less than truthful to pretend that gunfitting is a simple matter. It is part art and part craft, with few absolutes. If you have a serious problem, it obviously makes sense to seek out an expert. However, with a methodical approach and a bit of trial and error, and a friend to keep you in check, most competent shooters can work out basic alterations to their guns for themselves. I am going to set out, in no special order, some additional points which I think are useful:

Someone who stands square on the target, like Robert Churchill or George Digweed, will require a shorter stock with more cast than someone who adopts the oblique Stanbury/modified Stanbury stance.

Some Continental guns with very thick combs may show only a little cast at heel, but because of the thickness of the comb at face, they will effectively have no cast at all.

With a conventionally inclined comb, shortening or lengthening the stock will affect the drop measurement at face.

Ladies with large busts (and gentlemen with excess flesh on their chests), will need a gun with a rounded toe.

Guns for Sporting Clays and Skeet, where quick mounting is important, should have a rounded heel so as not to catch clothing. Similarly, guns fitted with rubber recoil pads may have the pads varnished or covered in leather (or even PVC tape) to prevent them from snagging.

People with long necks will find that a gun with approximately standard drop dimensions when mounted properly to the shoulder, will force them to cock their head down to make contact with the comb. They may be candidates for a Monte Carlo stock. With any individual, the comb should be sufficiently high so that when the gun is properly mounted, the head falls naturally against it without any need to cock the head down uncomfortably.

Adding or removing wood (or a recoil pad) will change the balance of a gun.

People who have chronic problems with face blistering and who do not respond to other remedies, may benefit from a stock that is altered so that it is parallel forward of the area of facial contact. Tapering the stock may also help, although I must also acknowledge that many face blistering problems are the result of poor gun mounting technique.

More detailed information on this subject is available in my book *Gunfitting: the Quest for Perfection*, published by the Sportsman's Press.

11 Customizing

Trigger Pull

Trigger pulls are much more important than generally realized. It affects the timing of the shot. Many shooters can adapt to a poorly fitting gun reasonably well, but find bad trigger pulls much harder to cope with. I notice this especially when I am testing guns. Although trigger pulls should be adjusted to personal preference, as long as they are within the safety limitations recommended by the manufacturer or gunsmith (for example, Beretta recommend no lighter than 3lb on the 68-series guns), there are some some general points worth noting:

1. All trigger pulls should be adjusted to break 'cleanly', without creep.
2. Heavy pulls may cause the shooter to pull-off target.
3. Generally, heavier guns will want slightly heavier pulls than lighter ones.
4. The second pull should be a little heavier than the first.

Typically, an 8lb boxlock over-and-under gun should be adjusted to about 3½lb for the first pull, 3¾lb for the second. However, my own preference is a little less than this – 3lb and 3¼lb. The best sidelocks, and over-and-unders like the Perazzi which, like sidelocks, use leaf rather than coil springs in the action, may be adjusted even lower – but only for Trap shooting. In Sporting, Skeet, and especially game, shooting, however, too light a trigger pull can be dangerous. I would never recommend less than 2¾lb on a Skeet or Sporting gun.

BALANCE

Where should a gun balance? Many will tell you that a shotgun should balance on its hinge-pin, others suggest that a gun swings more smoothly if it is balanced just forward of the hinge-pin. Good balance is hard to define. Sometimes it is stated that a well-balanced gun is one in which the weight is 'between the hands'. This is a typical characteristic of many best-quality sidelocks. Yet extraordinary feats of shooting have been accomplished by pump and semi-automatic shotguns which, to my mind at least, balance like old bits of drainpipe.

The balance requirements of a game gun are different from those of a clay gun. A game gun wants to be fairly lively, while a gun intended for Sporting or English or NSSA Skeet – where steadiness is essential for winning scores – wants to be both heavier, and more neutral in its balance characteristics. The Skeet gun especially may benefit from being a little muzzle-heavy too. Although a few formulas have been suggested for good balance, it all boils down to opinion. We react differently to the feel of different guns. I set up Sporters to balance on the hinge-pin if they are 28in or 30in barrelled, and about ⅛in forward of the hinge-pin centre if they have 32in tubes. I dislike guns that are noticeably muzzle- or stock-heavy for Sporting use.

Weight can be introduced into the stock by gluing lead in position, or by using heavy lead shot in putty. Weight may be taken from a stock by drilling or otherwise hollowing it (a skilled job). Weight can be added to barrels by using glaziers' lead strip (the type used for fake leaded windows). Weight can be taken from the barrels by overboring them (which has much to recommend it anyway since it decreases recoil and improves patterns – *see* page 149), and, at least on over-and-unders, by removing, partially removing, or lightening the joining ribs.

CHOKE

Choke – that is, the constriction of the bore at the muzzle of most shotgun barrels – was probably invented in the last century. There is some debate as to who was responsible for this. The American professional hunter Fred Kimble is most often cited as the father of choke boring and the great English gunmaker W.W. Greener is undoubtedly the man who popularized it. In 1875, Greener proved the superiority of choke at a public trial organized by the sporting journal *The Field*. The results caused a revolution in Sporting Gun manufacture.

There has been an enormous amount of argument over the years about what is the best choking for a gun. Some suggest very open chokes for Sporting shooting; others point out that although open chokes produce a wider pattern, tight chokes increase the shot-string effect and may be an advantage on longer crossing targets for that reason. It is hardly surprising that a lot of people cannot make up their minds: go to any shoot and you will observe those with multichoked guns obsessively changing tubes between stands (this seems even more of an illness in the United States, where one can even buy an electric choke-changer!).

For the great majority, changing chokes is a pointless exercise and acts only as a distraction. Some very successful Sporting shots use improved and ¼ (Michael Reynolds), or ¼ and ¼ for everything; ½ and ½ choke is good enough for all the Sporting and Skeet shooting of former World Sporting Champion John Bidwell; Percy Stanbury, the famous shooting instructor, used to have his old Webley 400 choked

full and full, and he used it for all the English disciplines with great success.

I believe this is the bottom line: some choke in a gun is important because it improves pattern consistency, especially at long range, but the need for widely different chokes for different birds is questionable, especially with the latest advances in barrel technology. I would generally recommend ½ and ½ for experienced shots (my own guns combine ½ and tight ½ with back-bored barrels and long forcing cones). A choke of ½ and ½ is wide enough to leave a little room for error, but it is not so wide as to tolerate sloppiness. With ½ and ½, one not only achieves good kills, but one also gets a very clear idea as to where one is killing the bird. Moreover, since there is little doubt that ½ and ½ will kill anything, one can stop worrying about technicalities, and get on with the essential business of watching the target.

For less experienced shots, I recommend improved and ¼, or ¼ and ¼. (If you are an incurable choke changer my advice is use open chokes when you can see the belly of the target and tighter chokes when it is edge on. Many say that rabbits require tighter chokes too, because the target is less brittle than a standard clay.)

So much for the degree of constriction, but the length of the choke is also becoming an area for debate. There is something of a rage at present for long chokes. This is supported by Browning (who have made long chokes their standard now) and by Nigel Teague who is one of the most knowledgeable people I know on the subject of chokes, and who has become well known for his multichoke conversions to fixed-choke guns.

Teague, a Rolls-Royce trained engineer, is convinced of the superiority of long chokes. His new chokes are 2¾in long and are all taper – that is, they do not have the parallel section that conventional chokes do. The purpose of the conical design is to reduce pellet deformation and improve pattern uniformity. I have certainly been impressed with the shooting characteristics of guns equipped with these chokes. They seem to require less constriction than guns that are conventionally choked, to achieve the same results. The new design has particular advantages for steel shot, which may damage the abrupt cones which lead into traditional chokes, and also for light-payload cartridges where the shooter cannot afford flyers outside the main body of the pattern.

It is important to understand that the patterns actually thrown by a gun do not necessarily correspond to the markings on chokes or barrels. It is often the case that the patterns

thrown by cheaper guns bear little relation to the marked constrictions. The only answer is to pattern your gun. I usually do this at both 25 and 40 yards. As a guide, at 40 yards a gun should pattern according to the percentage figures shown in the table opposite which are based on the number of pellets inside a 30-inch circle at that distance.

Choke percentages apart, a good pattern is one that is even without excessive central concentration, that has few gaps, and that shows no signs of pellet clustering. What really

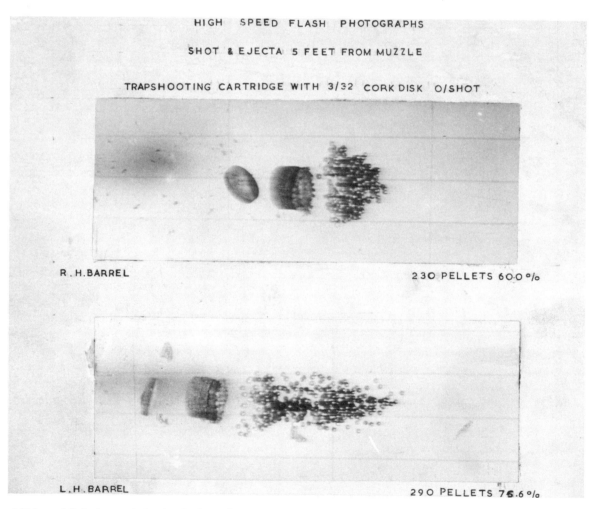

A high-speed flash photograph showing the shot and wad 5 feet (1.5m) from the muzzles in a lightly choked (top) and a heavily choked (bottom) barrel. Note the longer shot-string that is a consequence of heavier choking.

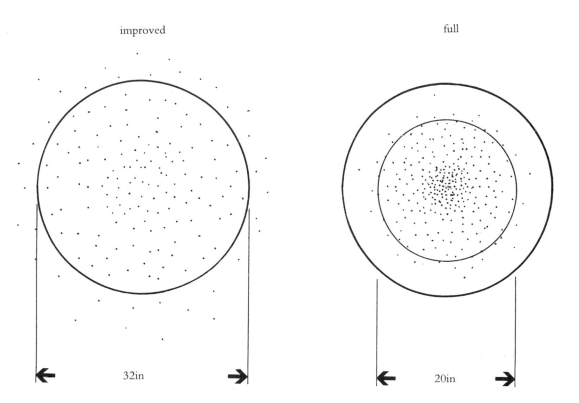

improved   full

32in   20in

The pattern from an improved cylinder barrel and a full-choke barrel at 25 yards (23m). Note: full choke is not only smaller but has greater central concentration.

counts, of course, are not percentage figures, but the way the gun breaks real targets. I know

of many guns which patterned poorly at plates but which killed targets impressively. And moreover, I know of many shooters, previously confident of their gun's performance, who would have been better off if they had never seen a pattern plate!

Traditional Choke for 12-Bores

Choke	Constriction
True cylinder	0
Improved cylinder	5
¼ choke	10
½ choke (Modified, USA)	20
¾ choke (improved modified, USA)	30
Full choke	40

Choke	Percentage inside 30-in circle
True cylinder	35–40
Improved cylinder	50
¼ choke	55
½ choke	60
¾ choke	65
Full choke	70 plus

NB Range 40 yards

CARTRIDGES

A shotgun cartridge consists of a case (usually plastic but sometimes paper) with a brass or steel-plated brass rim. In the centre of the rim is a primer, which creates a very small, controlled explosion at the bottom of the cartridge case when it is struck by the firing pin. This ignites the propellant powder (which is not an explosive) creating a lot of gas suddenly. The expanding gases drive a piston-like wad up through the case and into the barrel, pushing in front of it the shot charge.

Cartridges have improved a great deal over the years. Today, they use non-corrosive primer compounds (instead of mercury, which rotted barrels), and they no longer have rolled turnovers but use a crimp closure, which improves patterns. Felt and fibre wads are still used, but most modern cartridges use a plastic-skirted wad-cum-shot-cup which significatnly improves pattern quality. These wads form a more efficient gas seal, reduce damage to pellets as they travel up the bore, and also tend to tighten patterns slightly.

The propellant in most modern cartridges is nitro-cellulose, made from treating cotton with nitric acid. Some cartridges have a double-base powder which uses nitro-glycerine in the mix as well. Double-base powders burn better at low temperatures (an important practical consideration for those who shoot in the cold a lot). As far as shot is concerned, some modern cartridges use especially hard shot or plated shot to reduce pellet deformation. Hard shot tends to produce a better pattern, and is produced by alloying the lead with antimony.

Future Trends

Steel shot is likely to be forced on us one day, not least because the big American manufacturers have already made a huge investment in it owing to the legal requirement to use it for duck hunting in the United States. Steel is not as effective as lead at longer ranges because it does not retain kinetic energy so well. It's advantage is that it oxidizes harmlessly when deposited in earth or water. Whether there is a significant environmental danger from lead shot is dubious.

Steel shot can also cause significant wear in barrels, especially at the chokes. Research is being conducted currently into the possibility of using other metals for shot manufacture. Tungsten polymers have been tried and so has bismuth, which seems more promising. It is a heavy metal with similar properties to lead (including a low melting point) and is far less expensive than tungsten. It would still double the price of a box of cartridges, though.

Eco-consciousness also makes it likely that fibre wads, biodegradable, and photodegradable plastic wads (biodegradable plastic has an enzyme in it which accelerates the breakdown of the material, while photodegradable plastic is attacked by sunlight), or fibre wads with a

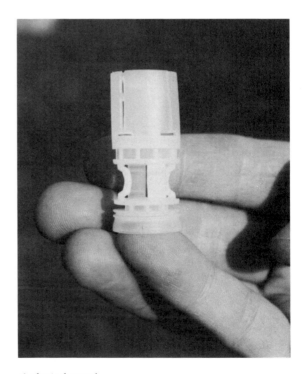

A plastic shot wad.

All sorts of opinions have been expressed as to the best sort of cartridges for Sporting shooting. My usual advice is to stick to 7½ shot for everything.

degradable skirt will become the norm one day. There is sound evidence to support the latter's introduction in that conventional plastic wads seem to have unpleasant effects on the bovine digestive system! Traditional fibre-wadded cartridges tend to be slower and pattern slightly wider than the equivalent plastic-wadded ones. The degradable wads perform in a very similar if not identical fashion to conventional plastic wads. They are a useful advance.

My philosophy with cartridges is much the same as my philosophy with choke. I know that I have missed far more targets because of bad gun mounting than because of poor or unsuitable cartridges or the wrong choke constriction. Most modern lead-shot cartridges are good. I would recommend 1oz of 7½ (US 8)

or 8 (no US equivalent) shot for all Sporting targets. My rationale is that I know that 7½s or 8s will break every target on a Sporting layout; 9s, with a smaller pellet and therefore less kinetic energy, just might not (though recently I shot a round of DTL with ⅞oz number 9 shotshells and shot 25-straight, with good kills as well. (9 shot seems to perform particularly well in the sub-1oz loads, which may be owed to the fact that, all other things being equal, it tends to increase pressure because it reduces the gaps between the pellets.)

Operating on the KISS principle, I do not want to waste a lot of energy and lose concentration considering what will or will not work from stand to stand, so I use 7½ or 8 for everything on serious shoots.

Theoretical Forward Allowance

Standard-velocity cartridge

30yd	35yd	40yd	45yd	50yd
5ft 6in	6ft 8in	8ft 0in	9ft 6in	11ft 1in

(1,070ft per second)

High-velocity cartridge

30yd	35yd	40yd	45yd	50yd
5ft 3in	6ft 5in	7ft 8in	9ft 1in	10ft 8in

(1,120ft per second)

(Information courtesy of Eley Hawk.)

I always recommend light-loaded cartridges to my students. I suspect that one day we shall find that recoil is much more dangerous than we currently realize (which is not to say that we are entirely unaware of the danger at present; recoil-induced neck and shoulder injuries among those who shoot a great deal are the reason the lighter loads for the Olympic disciplines have been introduced). The only potential problem with light loads is that the combustion of the propellant powder can be affected by cold weather. The problem is aggravated by felt wads and long forcing cones. Double-base powders may be part of the answer.

Is Cartridge Velocity Important?

Most clay shooters are now convinced of the merits of the 28g cartridge, and more and more are trying ultra-light loads. One consequence of the '1oz revolution' is that higher velocities are easy to achieve. I like quick cartridges as long as they are smooth to shoot. They seem to break the target more decisively. Do they reduce forward allowance? The difference between a high- and standard-velocity cartridge at forty yards is measured in inches, as the chart (above right) makes clear.

Reloading

I have nothing against reloading; it is an absorbing hobby in itself. If you want to learn about cartridges, take it up. However, do not fool yourself into thinking that you will save much money. By the time you take into consideration the cost of equipment and your time, reloading offers few, if any, savings (an exception is the reloading of 28-bore and .410 shells). As an economy measure, I do recommend that you band together with a couple of friends and buy cartridges in bulk.

EXCESSIVE RECOIL

Many shots seem willing to put up with more recoil than necessary, even though it is well established that excessive recoil is bad for you. Not only can it lead to bruising and headaches, but it can damage your neck vertebrae and shoulder. This is why clay shooting's governing bodies have been reducing the legal loads in some disciplines. (24g loads have recently been introduced in the UIT disciplines – Olympic Skeet and Trap. 28g (1oz) loads have been the rule for some time in English Sporting.)

What is the cause of recoil? Simple physics states that to every action there is an opposite and equal reaction. When a cartridge is fired, the combustion of the propellant powder creates gases as we have just noted. These raise the pressure inside the weapon, forcing the wad and shot charge down the barrel; the opposite reaction forces the gun back toward the shoulder.

The recoil of a gun may be measured in the laboratory when it is shot from a jig or cradle. Rearward acceleration is recorded. We call this actual or dynamic recoil (the latter term is Gough Thomas's). However, the shooter is most interested in felt recoil, which is the effect of actual recoil on his body. Guns that have similar actual recoil can have very different felt recoil for different individuals. This is because some people are more recoil-sensitive than others, and also because bodies of different shapes will interact with the same gun in different ways. Technique makes a big difference; someone who squashes his head down on the stock may well feel more recoil than someone who maintains a more upright head position. Similarly someone who lifts his head or holds the gun loosely may also be affected by recoil.

The two most common causes of kick are poor mounting technique and cartridges that are more powerful than they need to be. All sorts of other things can increase felt recoil though: a steeply inclined stock comb, too short a stock, a stock with a prominent toe, too much cast, a lightweight gun, a gun which is 'off the face' (in which the barrels and action are not properly jointed), a gun which has excessive headspace (one cause of which is too great a rim depth in the chamber), a gun which has chambers that are too large, a gun in which the bore diameter is too tight (most guns start life at .729 – beware those that measure .719), a gun with tight chokes, a gun which has short forcing cones in front of its chambers, and, not least, a gun with a poorly shaped grip or fore-end (the hands absorb a great deal of recoil).

There is a wide variety of products available to reduce recoil (though many more are available in the US than in the UK). These include a vast array of recoil pads (the ventilated-

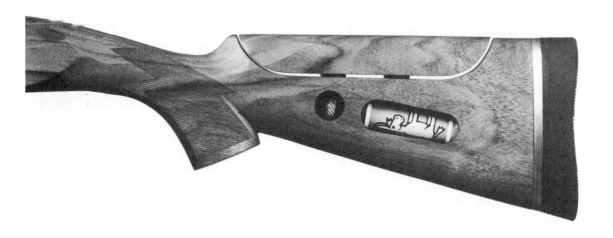

This stock is equipped with a recoil-reducer and also an adjustable comb and bad. (Photograph by courtesy of Alan Rhone.)

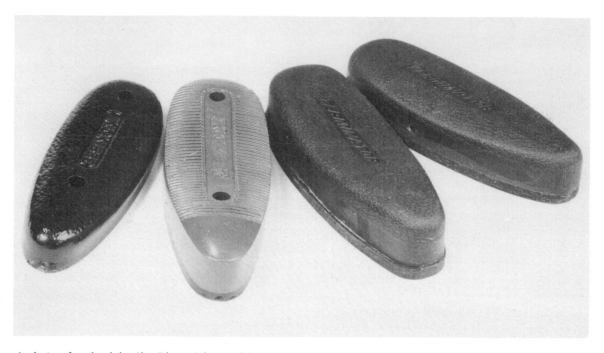

A selection of recoil pads by Alan Rhone. (Photograph by courtesy of Alan Rhone.)

A rear view of an adjustable pad. (Photograph by courtesy of Alan Rhone.)

trap types and those made of Sorbothane are especially effective), and varous inertial devices designed to be fitted into the stock (or occasionally, in repeaters, inside the magazine tube) to dampen recoil. Some utilize a piston in a tube, some are simply metal tubes filled with mercury. The efficacy of such devices, which typically weigh half a pound or more, may have as much to do with the extra weight they introduce into the gun than with any magical action of their internal mechanics. Getting a step more complex is the telescoping Hydro-Coil stock. It turns the stock into an air-dampened shock-absorber; it works very well and has been imitated by several companies. Barrels may also be customized to reduce recoil in various ways. The bores may be enlarged; this is called 'overboring' or 'backboring' (*see* page 149), the forcing cones can be lengthened (*see* page 149), and porting holes or slots may be cut at the end of the barrel tubes (*see* page 150). The first two modifications may also improve pattern quality.

The Hydro-Coil stock uses an air-damping system and turns the whole stock into a telescopic shock-absorber.

Overboring

Most 12-bore guns are made about .729in in internal diameter (though some are significantly tighter). An overbored gun might be opened up to .755in or more. Before undertaking the modification, the gunsmith will make sure that the wall thickness of the barrels is adequate. After modification, which may also include attention to the chokes to match the new bore, the gun will need to be re-proofed.

Overboring reduces friction in the barrel. It appears to reduce velocity, (although more scientific work needs to be done). It can also have a beneficial effect on pattern quality. The positive effects are most noticeable when a gun is firing heavy charges.

After much experimentation, I have come to the conclusion that .740–.745 (plus 10,000 or 15,000 on the typical standard dimension) is the ideal bore diameter for a Sporting gun; larger diameters than this can cause problems related to inadequate pressure with lightly loaded cartridges, especially in cold weather, and with felt-wadded cartridges. The cold affects the combustion of the propellant powder, reducing chamber pressure; the problem is aggravated with felt wads (which have a less efficient gas seal), and by long forcing cones.

Lengthening Forcing Cones

The forcing cone is the funnel-like construction in front of the chamber. It directs the

149

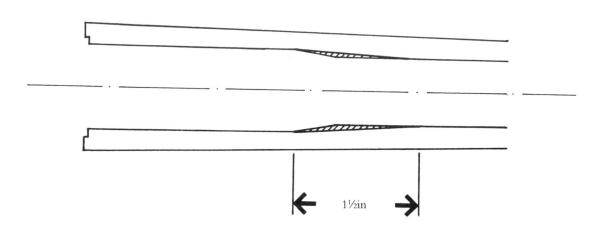

The funnel-like forcing cone constriction and how it may be lengthened.

shot and wad into the main bore of the gun. In the days of rolled-over cartridges and felt wads, a short, abrupt cone was needed to maintain adequate chamber pressures. With today's much more efficient cases, wads and powders, this is not the case and a fashion has developed for lengthening forcing cones. Longer cones seem to reduce perceived recoil and make a gun smoother to shoot. How do they work? It appears that they prevent the wad and shot from being abused too much as they enter the main body of the bore. They may also reduce chamber pressure.

The big question is, how long should forcing cones be? Many guns have been converted to 2in, but 1½in can be considered standard. As one of those who started the fad in the UK, I have had the chance to shoot many converted guns. My conclusions are that 1½in should be considered a maximum; if you use ultra-light cartridges (below 28g) or fibre wads, go for something shorter, no longer than 1¼in.

As with overboring, cold weather, light cartridges and long cones do not mix. I also tend to the view that one should stick with a 1¼in maximum for any gun with open chokes. However, I acknowledge that this is, essentially,

guesswork; much more scientific analysis needs to be done in this area of shotgun ballistics.

Porting

A ported gun directs some of the propellant gases upwards, thus reducing muzzle flip and, for some users, felt recoil. Porting also helps speed target acquisition for the second shot.

The effects of porting are very noticeable when they are explored with slow motion photography; muzzle flip is reduced by about 50 per cent. Subjectively, though, I cannot feel much difference between ported and non-ported guns. Moreover, ported guns have certain disadvantages. They require a little extra effort to clean. More importantly, they can suffer from a mirage effect on the rib, because the hot gases leaving the porting holes heat up the front portion of the rib more than a non–ported gun. Another potential problem with some ported guns is noise, although this can be minimized by ensuring that the number of holes used is not excessive.

If you do suffer from recoil, get a good instructor to check your technique and change to a light-loaded cartridge before you start modifying your gun.

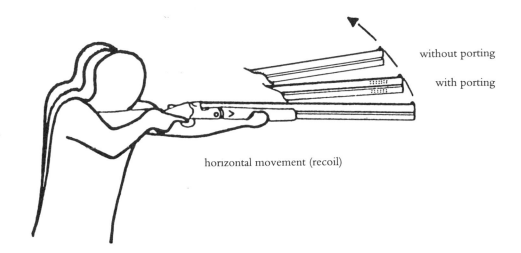

Horizontal movement recoil, with and without porting. (Illustration by courtesy of Gunmark Ltd.)

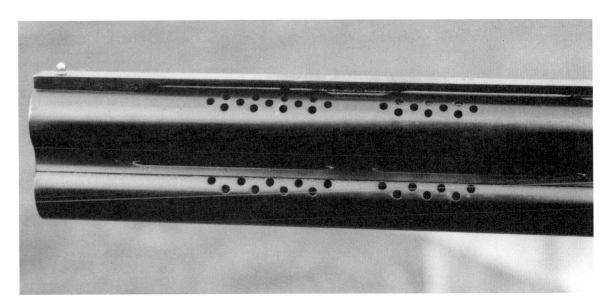

A ported gun. Note that more holes are used on the top barrel.

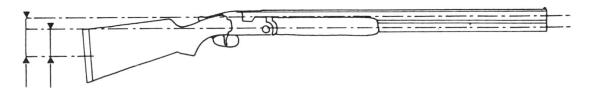

This drawing shows why the top barrel of an over-and-under can cause more muzzle flip than the bottom barrel. (Illustration by courtesy of Gunmark Ltd.)

Flinching

Flinching, an involuntary muscle spasm in anticipation of the gun going off, affects some shooters, and can be a very serious problem. Whether it starts initially because of a subconscious fear of gunblast or simply in physical response to a painful stimulus, I am not sure. I do know that once the problem sets in, it gradually gets worse and can lead some people to give up shooting altogether.

If you suspect you have a flinch, the first thing to do – if it is not immediately obvious – is to test for it. This is simply done by getting someone to load for you while you turn your head to one side: he will load only one cartridge without your knowing which chamber it is in. (If you have a gun with a leaf-spring action, a snap cap should be used in the other chamber.) Shoot as normal, at a simple target twice. If you have a flinch, it will be immediately apparent when the hammer falls on the snap cap. The violence of the involuntary body movement is quite surprising. If you have a flinch, you must then ask why have you acquired it. Does your gun fit? Are you using cartridges that cause too much recoil? Is your mounting technique poor? Are you very tired?

You will have to sort these problems out (if in doubt, seek professional help). You will also have to unlearn the negative psychomuscular response.

There are various ways to do this. You may work with snap caps every weekday night for a month or so, going through a practice routine as described elsewhere in this book and actually pulling the trigger as the gun swings with the imaginary target. You must do this again and again and again, until you get nothing but a sense of comfort and well-being when you pull the trigger. You might also buy an air rifle, preferably of the non-recoiling type, and shoot it at least twenty-five times a day for a month or so. Gradually, you will break the flinching response, as you learn that a trigger can be pulled without fear or pain. When you are satisfied that the habit is gone, return to shooting (I would suggest that a minimum of a one month lay-off is part of the cure for flinching), and consider using nothing but sub-ounce loads for a while. If need be, change your gun to something known for its reduced recoil.

Do not allow yourself to shoot too much; concentrate on quality rather than quantity. I am convinced that many experienced shooters

An air rifle – one cure for flinching. (Photograph by courtesy of Guns and Shooting *magazine.)*

acquire a flinch in the first place simply because they shoot too much. They get in the habit of shooting even when they are physically tired. Release triggers are sometimes suggested as a cure for flinching (especially in the United States), but they are not suited to Sporting shooting, and do not address the fundamental problem.

12 Conclusions

This book has covered a great many subjects. I have made the point already that safety and a good gun mount are overwhelmingly important. As an instructor I see hundreds of people annually who think that they are safe and competent when they are far from it. If you start from the assumption that you are less than perfect, you can only get better. The problem is

No matter your level of ability, every shot can benefit from professional instruction. The attitude which admits that learning is a continual process is part of the attitude that wins.

This shooter shows good style and is clearly in control of the gun. She is also having fun: good shooting requires discipline, but enjoying yourself is important, too.

that shooting is such an ego sport that people seem unwilling or incapable of doing this. Some of them succeed in spite of a bad attitude,

but I am convinced they never realize their true potential or get the enjoyment and satisfaction from their sport that they otherwise might.

One can never really learn to shoot well without mastering the basics; and you must return to work on them regularly throughout your shooting career. The problem is that putting in the ground work can be very dull unless you have the right mental approach. I take a real pleasure in doing small things well. I think that is the essence of ultimate performance. Conversely, I cringe when I see someone slam a gun shut, or attempt to shoot with a cigarette in hand.

In *Positive Shooting* I have attempted to set down what I have learned in the last twenty-five years. In summing up, my best advice is for you to understand – but not to become too worried about – your equipment, practise regularly using a sound technique, and practise on hard targets in the company of good shots. Do not shoot too much. The definition of too much is when you have to shoot without being able to put total effort into every shot. Set goals in training. Develop a routine. Take pride in what you do. You may miss targets on occasion, but you can make the decision now always to shoot well. Hit or miss, but do it with style. In the long run, good style will lead to good scores. Finally, always remember the golden rule: *watch* and *keep watching* the target!

Further Reading

Bentley, Paul, *Competitive Clay Target Shooting*, A & C Black, London (1991)

Bidwell, John, with Scott, Robin, *Move, Mount, Shoot*, The Crowood Press, Marlborough (1990).

Blatt, Art, *The Gun Digest Book of Trap & Skeet Shooting*, DBI Books Inc., Illinois, (1984).

Bowlen, Bruce, *The Orvis Wing-Shooting Handbook*, Nick Lyons Books, New York (1985).

Brister, Bob, *Shotgunning: The Art and the Science*, Winchester Press, Oklahoma (1976).

Churchill, Robert, *Game Shooting*, Michael Joseph, London (1963).

   How to Shoot, reprinted by The Sportsman's Press, London (1988).

Cradock, Chris, *A Manual of Clayshooting*, B.T. Batsford, London, (1988).

Davies, Ken, *The Better Shot*, Quiller Press, London (1992).

Greener, W.W., *The Gun and its Development*, Arms and Armour Press Ltd., London (1986).

Lancaster, Charles, *The Art of Shooting*, Ashford Press Publishing, Southampton (1985).

Martin, Dr Wayne, *An Insight to Sports Featuring Trapshooting and Golf*, Sportsvision Inc., Seattle (1984).

Ohye, Kaye, *You and the Target*, Scattergun Press, Texas (1987).

Reynolds, Mike, with Barnes, Mike, *Shooting Made Easy*, The Crowood Press, Marlborough (1986.

The Rules of Proof, HMSO, London (1989).

Scherer, Ed, *Scherer on Skeet II*, Ed Scherer, Wisconsin (1991).

Smith, A.J., *Sporting Clays Master Class*, Argus, Hemel Hempstead (1991).

Stanbury, Percy and Carlisle, G.L., *Clay Pigeon Marksmanship*, Barrie & Jenkins, London (1982).

Thomas, Gough, *Gun Book*, A & C Black, London (1983).

   Shotguns and Cartridges for Game and Clays, A & C Black, London (1975).

Yardley, Michael, *Gunfitting: The Quest for Perfection*, The Sportsman's Press, London (1993).

Zutz, Don, *Shotgunning: Trends in Transition*, Wolfe Publishing Co., Arizona (1989).

Rule books for Sporting and other disciplines are available from the Clay Pigeon Shooting Association (CPSA). (*See* Useful Addresses.)

Useful Addresses

London Proof House
48 Commercial Road
London
E1 1LP

Birmingham Proof House
Banbury Street
Birmingham
B5 5RH

United States National Sporting Clays
    Association
P.O. Box 680007
San Antonio
Texas, 78268

Clay Pigeon Shooting Association (CPSA)
107 Epping New Road
Buckhurst Hill
Essex
IG9 5TQ

British Association for Shooting and
    Conservation (BASC)
Marford Mill
Rossett
Wrexham
Clwyd
LL12 0HL

Index